Where Murderers Walk Free

Jerry C. Berry

Order this book online at www.trafford.com/08-1002
or email orders@trafford.com

Most Trafford titles are also available at major online book retailers.

© Copyright 2008 Jerry C. Berry.

All rights reserved. No part of this publication may be reproduced, stored in a retrieval system, or transmitted, in any form or by any means, electronic, mechanical, photocopying, recording, or otherwise, without the written prior permission of the author.

Edited by: Susan E. Berry

Note for Librarians: A cataloguing record for this book is available from Library and Archives Canada at www.collectionscanada.ca/amicus/index-e.html

Printed in Victoria, BC, Canada.

ISBN: 978-1-4251-8483-4

We at Trafford believe that it is the responsibility of us all, as both individuals and corporations, to make choices that are environmentally and socially sound. You, in turn, are supporting this responsible conduct each time you purchase a Trafford book, or make use of our publishing services. To find out how you are helping, please visit www.trafford.com/responsiblepublishing.html

Our mission is to efficiently provide the world's finest, most comprehensive book publishing service, enabling every author to experience success. To find out how to publish your book, your way, and have it available worldwide, visit us online at www.trafford.com/10510

www.trafford.com

North America & international
toll-free: 1 888 232 4444 (USA & Canada)
phone: 250 383 6864 ♦ fax: 250 383 6804
email: info@trafford.com

The United Kingdom & Europe
phone: +44 (0)1865 487 395 ♦ local rate: 0845 230 9601
facsimile: +44 (0)1865 481 507 ♦ email: info.uk@trafford.com

10 9 8 7 6 5 4 3 2

FROM THE AUTHOR:

All matters involving each investigation in this book are based on my personal exposure to each case file and my own involvement.

I will make no attempt to soften the nature of homicide investigations as I walk the reader through each step of the investigations. I will leave it to the reader to draw a conclusion at the end of each story, based on the evidence provided.

I would also like to express my deepest sympathy to the surviving family members of the victims who lost their lives to violent criminal activity. I am especially sorry to the victims whose murderers were not brought to justice. The victims and their families will forever be a part of me.

Former Detective Jerry C. Berry

Disclaimer

On all cases that were not cleared with an arrest and conviction, names were changed to protect the innocent. Any suspects in these cases will be the opinion of the reader derived from the reader's own conclusion based on the information contained herein.

DEDICATION

I dedicate this book to the families who have lost loved ones, to the victims who were faced with the evil side of humanity, and to all those who lost loved ones due to botched and poorly conducted investigations.

Acknowledgements

I don't believe that I would have ever completed this book had it not been for the support and encouragement of the following individuals. Words cannot adequately express the gratitude and appreciation I have for their devotion and loyalty.

To my mother, Bernice Berry, whose gentle encouragement in reminding me of the importance of the truth being told, and the need for the citizens to know the consequences of poorly conducted investigations. Unfortunately she passed away January 24, 2006 and never got to see this book in print.

To my wife Susan, who has never wavered in her belief in me. She is a constant inspiration to me, and she worked tirelessly editing the many manuscripts. She has encouraged me to continue in my attempts to make Lewis County a better place, by exposing the deception and false impressions created by some elected officials.

To my best friends Mike and Jeanne Pea, who were always there to lend advice and encouragement. Mike is one of the few deputies who had the courage to stand beside me and openly show his support.

To my friends and former law enforcement officers, Micheal and Carol Hurley, who spent hours assisting in the editing process of this book.

Foreword

Standing by your principles can sometimes be tough for a lawman, particularly if you happen to be on the wrong side of the issue.

It doesn't matter that you happen to be right. What matters is how you play the game. Jerry Berry didn't play by the same rules as some of those at the Lewis County Sheriff's Office. He was more interested in getting the job done right, than just getting the job done.

The woman was dead. Jerry's job was to find out why and how. Was it complacency or had laziness set in with some of his fellow investigators? In this day of hang it on the cops and pay the criminals, who can really blame them? But to Jerry it was charge forward, fall on his sword, if he must, but try his hardest to bring to justice those who trampled on our most cherished right; the right to live.

Cold blooded killers do not play by the Marcus of Queensbury rules, but the cops must. Jerry was in a fight with one hand tied behind him by a criminal justice system that is more concerned with how the cops play the game, rather than the innocence or guilt of the suspect.

Imagine arriving at the scene of a murder to find the crime scene soiled by a group of citizens or lawmen who thought it was okay to check things out. Sometimes just determining that the victim is actually dead will contaminate the crime scene. But "Show and Tell" at a crime scene is strictly forbidden for the sake of preserving evidence.

Nowhere in the United States Constitution does it say that a lawman has to have a search warrant before he or she conducts a search. It only says a search has to be reasonable. But the lawmen, who we trust to carry a gun and give a license to kill, aren't deemed qualified enough to determine when a search fits the legal definition of reasonable. It takes a learned judge who doesn't have a clue about what the probable cause is, but must rely on the written word of, yes, a cop who has to stop in the middle of his investigation to write up an affidavit and a search warrant for the judge to read. Guess what? That won't be the end of it. That affidavit and search warrant will have to stand the test of time as it becomes fodder for arguments up and down the legal system until finally the nine Justices of the United States Supreme Court decide by a vote, of five to four, that the cop should have done something differently.

So, we have four of the most influential, if not learned, judges in the country that decided the cop was right in the first place, so why all the hassle? Well, that's just the way it is. And, it is for that reason Jerry Berry was trying to be meticulous in his gathering and preservation of evidence.

In spite of all the obstacles, Jerry fought a good fight, and this, his story, puts you up close and personal in a ride-along with a homicide detective who is hell bent on catching the culprit.

Micheal T. Hurley (DEA-Ret.) Author of *I Solemnly Swear*

1
The Early Days

CHASING DOWN MURDERERS as a career never entered my mind when I started out in the work force so many years ago. Little did I know that years later I would be involved in a murder investigation that would become very controversial and high profile. I didn't go looking for a law enforcement position, but stepped into one by happenstance.

I spent the first 22 years of my working life as a union carpenter. I did it by choice and made a good living at it. I know what hard work is and I know what it means to finish a job with some sense of pride. I started working heavy construction at the age of 17 but, by the age of 39, I found that I was getting tired of the back-breaking physical labor and wanted to do something else. I really didn't know what I was going to do, but I knew I was going to find something.

One day in August, 1989, I was in Mossyrock Market at the checkout counter. Like most small communities, you know everyone and people take the time to talk to each other. Knute, the store owner and I were talking about the town Marshal who was standing on the sidewalk across the street. Billy (not his real name) had been appointed to the position of Marshal by the town Mayor. By state law, after an appointment to a law enforcement position, the appointee has to pass the physical entry exam and the Basic Law Enforcement Academy. It was very unlikely that Billy could do either one of those things.

Billy knew little to nothing about law enforcement and just flew by the seat of his pants, administering his own brand of justice. How the City kept from getting sued is beyond me. Just the appearance of

Billy when he was on duty told most people that local law enforcement was in serious trouble. This was the topic of the conversation between Knute and me.

Billy was standing on the sidewalk talking to one of the local bar patrons in his usual attire. He was wearing old Levis and a pair of run-down tennis shoes. His tan khaki shirt had one tail tucked in and the other one hanging out, with the top two buttons left undone. His blond curly hair was several months past a cut and probably hadn't seen a comb in as long. A two-week growth of beard covered his face and I don't ever recall him without it. If this image of local law enforcement wasn't bad enough, the way he wore his badge and gun completed the picture; an old 22 caliber six shot revolver tucked into a worn western style holster hung from his neck by a leather shoestring. This placed the holstered weapon just below the badge pinned to his shirt pocket.

In defense of Billy, he was doing the job the only way he knew how, considering he had no training or law enforcement education. He had been placed into the position by the Mayor, handed a badge, and turned loose. You have to understand small towns and communities, such as are found in areas like Lewis County, are often run by the "old timers" who still see everything as they did 50 years ago. They never seem to quite make it into the present century.

I remember making the comment to Knute that "I could do a better job than Billy, and I don't know anything about the law!" Knute's response was, "Then why don't you go across the street and talk to the Mayor." This sounded a lot like a challenge to me so I said, "I think I will." And that is how I found myself embarking on a career in law enforcement that would change my life forever.

James Robetts owned the local liquor store and had been around forever. He and Billy were part of the "good ole boy" faction in the area. You would recognize the group because every town has one. Seems like they are always operating a half century behind the rest of the world and everything is their way or the highway. James was sitting behind the counter on a stool reading a newspaper when I walked in; the usual cloud of cigar smoke hung thick in the air. The smoke was so think that it all but obscured the liquor bottles that lined the shelves behind him. "Hey James, I want to apply for the Marshal's job" I said, squinting from the stinging in my eyes caused by the cigar smoke. "You got any experience?" he asked. "No, but I am in good shape and I can get through the academy" I told him. This seemed to be enough so he pulled out an application from under the counter. Regardless of anything else, I owe him for the opportunity he gave me.

After the Lewis County Sheriff's Office completed my background investigation, James notified me and told me that he was going to hire me and send me to the academy.

I knew that I was going to have a hard time at the academy because of what had happened with the previous cadet James had sent. The cadet before me had lied about his background. It didn't take long for the truth to come out at the academy and he was kicked out. Mossyrock had pretty much become the laughing stock of the State, and certainly was one of the favorite topics at the Washington State Criminal Justice Training Center (WSCJTC). I knew I was starting from the rear of the pack so to speak, plus I was starting at the age of 39. Now 39 seems young but, at the time, it was considered too old to be beginning a career in law enforcement. My years of active training in the martial arts would prove to be the key to my success, in more ways than one.

The first day I arrived at the hotel in Burien, Washington and met my roommates, I got a preview of what I could expect for awhile. One of the guys was quick to ask if I was a fag since I was from Mossyrock. I told them that I was from Mossyrock but I was no "fag" and I had kicked guy's asses for calling me less. The man apologized for offending me and then they told me what they had heard about Mossyrock. Because of the incredible turnover of police chiefs and the failures at the academy, Mossyrock had become the talk of the law enforcement community.

The next morning during our first inspection, when the Commander stopped in front of me, I got the feeling I was being sized up far more than the others. The commander asked me if I was the recruit from Mossyrock. I replied that I was, and after a few seconds of uncomfortable eye contact, he said, "well, good luck." Having Mossyrock's reputation of being a joke in the area of law enforcement, along with the problems created at the academy by the last recruit, I was even more determined to succeed. The next three months were grueling, but I finished in the top 5% percentile of the class and had won the respect of my peers and the academy staff, as well.

My martial arts skills quickly put me at the top of the defensive tactics class and the years of physical conditioning paid big dividends during the physical fitness tests. The "Old Man" in the class quickly became the Old Man the younger cadets came to after class for additional physical fitness and defensive tactics training. I never turned anyone down, even though it often resulted in me staying up later at night to get my studies done. The day before our final physical fitness test, I severely injured my left ankle during a training exercise. I made my teammates promise to keep it quiet and not say anything to the academy staff. If the staff found out, I would have been required to seek medical attention that same evening and would have not been allowed to participate in the final exam the next day. I had worked too hard and overcome too much at this point to be denied a chance to graduate with my class. There was no way I was going to let the Mayor and the town of Mossyrock down and be the topic of ridicule again!

The next morning when I got up, I wrapped my swollen ankle tight with ace bandages to eliminate as much movement as possible. I forced myself to walk without limping, at least when there was anyone around who would notice. After breakfast and some classroom instructions, it was time to head out to the track for our final physical fitness test. The test consisted of one lap around the quarter mile track as fast as we could go, one cadet at a time. Half way down the back side of the track was a six foot high wooden wall that we had to go over, then on through the first turn. Just before entering into the second straight away, there was a culvert we had to belly crawl through, then stand up and start running down the home stretch. About ¾ of the way through the straight stretch was a 10 foot high chain link fence that we had to get over, then a short distance to the finish line. Failure to make it through any portion was a failure of the test, and no graduation!

I remember how pumped up I was when I took off, heading for the six foot wooden wall. My ankle was on fire as I ran and as I went over the wall I made sure to land on my right foot. I made it around the west end of the track and was more than happy to belly crawl through the culvert; a chance to get off my feet for a few seconds. But, when I came out of the culvert, I made the mistake of lunging off from my left foot. The pain was like a burning rod being shoved into my ankle! I was running the best I could but there was no way to keep from limping or favoring the left foot. I remember how insurmountable the 10 foot high chain link fence appeared as I approached it. My ankle was on fire and I was gritting my teeth from the pain and I knew the chain link fence was going to either make or break my chances of graduation. When I was close enough, I lunged upward, pushing off as hard as I could with my right foot and leg. I grabbed the chain link and pulled my self upward, hand over hand, drawing from every ounce of reserve I had left, until I could throw my left leg over the top. I let my self down about half way then let go, trying to take all the weight on my right leg when I landed. I got up and tried to run but could only painfully hobble the short distance to the finish line and I just collapsed on the ground when I crossed it, my chest heaving as I tried to suck in enough air, my ankle on fire.

Later, my Tack Officer chewed me out for not telling him about my injury, but I knew that I had his respect for not quitting, and I graduated with my class!

2

THE NEW HIRE

"THEY CALL ME Baby Huey" was how Erick Hendrickson introduced himself to me.

While at the academy, I met and became good friends with Erick who actually turned 21 years old just weeks before we graduated. Erick lived in Longview, Washington, which is on the I-5 corridor about 40 miles north of Portland, Oregon. His goal was to eventually get hired by the Longview Police Department. The best chance for him to get hired was to apply as a lateral entry officer. To meet lateral requirements, he needed at least 12 months experience as a full time commissioned officer after graduation from the academy.

Erick had paid his own way through the Basic Law Enforcement Academy, and didn't have a job to go to when he graduated. I knew I was going to need help in bringing real law enforcement to the town of Mossyrock, and what better way to start than to have a young academy graduate with me. He had a good head on his shoulders and was very mature for a 21-year-old. Erick stood six foot, 2 inches and weighed in at 220 pounds. He had a round, jovial face and was always smiling, which gave him a very boyish appearance. The babyish face and passive demeanor won him the nickname "Baby Huey." He sported this nickname proudly in the form of a personalized license plate, "HUEY," on his powder blue Camaro.

He also had the same passion for law enforcement that I did, and was morally a good person. About four weeks before we were to graduate, I hired him as my only full- time officer.

Mossyrock, Washington is a small rural community with a population of less than 1000. Like many small communities, it has one main street on which the businesses are established, then several side streets comprised of private residences. It rests along State Route 12 about 20 miles East of Interstate 5, and has the distinction of having two large hydroelectric dams near by. Mayfield Lake sits just to the West of town and Riffe Lake sits just to the East, both attracting tourists and recreation-seeking citizens from around the State.

We had our hands full when we took control of the Police Department in Mossyrock. There had been virtually no respect for the law prior to us, and those who had no respect for the law, did just about whatever they wanted to do. The local taverns were, and always had been, a gathering place for the locals. Anything could and did occur in them, and they were the source of most of the problems in the community. They became our first target, or project, as I liked to call it.

We had a simple philosophy then, and that was to go to the source of the problems in the community. At the time, it was the taverns. Dope deals, fights and constant problems of over-serving were nightly events. So, Erick and I made a point to go into the taverns on a regular basis and make our presence known. We then parked at various locations and waited for the drunks to start driving off after closing. There was no shortage of drunk drivers; I even got one guy on a farm tractor. It took about one year for the criminal element to get the idea that professional law enforcement had finally come to town. No matter what the teen punks did, or what the tavern produced, we were always right there, and we solved almost every crime committed in town that year. They couldn't beat us and we weren't going away! According to a report released by the D.U.I. Task Force Coordinator, Don Younghan, drunk driving arrests increased by 400% in Mossyrock by the end of our first year.

Shortly after completing his first year with me, Erick tested for and was offered a job with the Longview Police Department. His dream was being fulfilled and he was finally going to have a chance to be an officer in his home town. He had proven to be a very capable officer. I was sad when he left, but I was glad to have been there to give him his first job as a police officer. We still talk occasionally on the phone and we will always remain friends.

3

THE CHANGE

IN MAY OF 1991, I was offered a position with the Lewis County Sheriff's Office as a Patrol Deputy. I had served the citizens of Mossyrock for nineteen months, which was longer that the 12 months I had promised them. There is nowhere to go and no way to grow in a two-man department. Money was certainly no incentive to stay, and there is nothing worse than "small town politics" and the small town mentality. I am the type that needs continual growth in any field or profession I choose to be a part of. That is why I jumped at the chance to work for the County.

Lewis County sits in the Southwest portion of the State of Washington. It covers approximately 2,435.5 square miles of some of the roughest, mountainous terrain in the State. Interstate 5 runs North and South through the middle of it. State Route 12 runs East and West through the middle of the county. These two major arterial highways are the primary transport routes through the county. Portland, Oregon sits just an hour and a half drive to the South and Seattle about the same to the North. SR 12 provides the route from the coast to the East side of the State. Chehalis and Centralia, known as "The Twin Cities" serve as the hub, with Chehalis being the County Seat. These two cities are the largest in the county with a total county population of about 68,600. The rest of the county consists of numerous small communities that struggle for existence since the logging industry started its decline during the mid 80's. The communities are spread from one end of the county to the other so that you can barely travel 10 miles without reaching one of them. Between each community there are farms and a huge amount of timberland, mostly owned by the big companies, like Weyerhaeuser, Champion and some by the Department of Natural Resources. This makes for an incredible amount of wilderness area and hard to reach secluded spots. These factors, along with I-5 and SR12 make the area a very attractive place for the criminal element to hide out and carry on their business. The methamphetamine industry was, and still is, booming in the county. At the time I quit the Lewis County Sheriff's Office, Lewis County was known by many around the State as, "The Meth. Capital of the State." There are a lot of decent law abiding citizens in Lewis County, but there are an unacceptable number of those who choose to live outside the rules and laws of society. The two main contributing factors I believe, is its remoteness and insufficient number of deputies to adequately patrol it.

The Lewis County Sheriff's Office has the responsibility of providing law enforcement throughout the county. When I left the Department, the Patrol Division consisted of about 50 deputies who were responsible for patrolling and investigating complaints for the county. The Detective Division consisted of the Detective Sergeant and four Detectives. Sadly, this is the same size the Division was during the early 1970's. It has never increased to match the county's growth and, in my opinion from my exposure to it, has never progressed in skill or technology.

Part of the hiring process with the Lewis County Sheriff's Office involved a one-on-one meeting with the Undersheriff. I remember my first meeting with the Undersheriff. He is a slim fellow, wears glasses, and at the time he had short, permed hair. This resulted in very tight little curls that created a lot of comical conversations within the Department. The meeting was, as far as I could tell, his time to let me know about his concerns, I guess. He specifically said to me, "You know your age is a concern". It seemed to me that he was precariously close to age discrimination, but I responded by telling him that I was probably in better shape than anyone in the Department. I remember thinking to myself at the time, "I know for sure I'm in better shape than you."

For the next four years, I worked hard to show my worth and my abilities as an investigator. I was one of a few deputies who rarely referred cases to the Detective Division. I worked the cases myself, doing the follow up work needed, and the results were a large number of arrests and convictions. If I was working traffic detail, then I wanted to be the best. I would write more tickets, arrest more drunk drivers, and impound more cars than my peers who worked the East end of the county with me. I figured the best way to become really good at something, was to jump in and get the hands-on experience.

From: Chief Criminal Deputy, Gordan Spanski
To: Deputy Jerry Berry
Subject: Seat Belt Enforcement in 1991

"I would like to commend you for the outstanding job you did in enforcing the restraint laws in 1991. You can be proud of the safety record you have achieved by actively pursuing this issue. The number of seat belt citations and warnings you issued make you one of the top performers of our department. I will be forwarding your name to the Washington State Traffic Commission for special recognition.
Keep up the good work"

4

THE ASSIGNMENT

AFTER TWO YEARS of applying and waiting, I was finally assigned to the Detective Division. Even though it was only a two-year assignment, I was excited to get the chance to work some big cases. I was given three one-year extensions to stay in the Detective Division due to my performance, for a total of 5 years.

I had worked several very large theft cases, as well as drug cases, with a high degree of success, but I wanted to work a murder case. My success in solving cases had gotten the attention of the Department and was a determining factor in being selected for the Detective assignment. Every investigation I conducted, regardless of the nature, I went to great lengths to study the crime scene. I learned early on to trust in "Locard's Theory;" that something is always taken from a scene and something is always left behind. A suspect will always leave something of himself. Whether it is a fingerprint, shoe print, blood, or something as small as a hair or fiber, something will be left. The same applies to taking something away, such as a trace of the victim's blood, skin tissue, hair, or fibers from the victim.

For the next several years, I never passed up an opportunity to attend any type of investigative training, and would apply for every class or seminar that came along. I read books, researched on the internet, and talked to professionals from various states whenever the opportunity arose. Anything that pertained to homicide investigations or crime scene interpretation, I wanted it. By the time I had been in the Detective Division three years, I had attended some very sophisticated seminars and obtained countless hours of training. Most of these were taught by national experts in their respective fields. Some of those, and probably the best were the following:

"*Advanced Homicide Investigations/Crime Scene Interpretation*" taught by Bob Keppel.

Doctor Keppel is best known for his participation in the Ted Bundy and Green River Killer investigations. He is one of the last investigators to interview Ted Bundy at the Florida prison before Bundy was executed. He is the author of several books on the subject of serial killers and homicide investigations. He has been consulted in several high profile investigations across the United States, and his name is well known in the circle of professional death investigators. His advanced class required me to drive just over 100 miles one way, two nights a week for eleven weeks. These trips were done after a full day at the Sheriff's Office, but they were well worth it. Attention to detail, never assuming anything, and thorough analytical evaluation of the entire crime scene were taught in detail.

"*Practical Homicide Investigations*" taught by Vernon Geberth.

Mr. Geberth retired from the New York City Police Department as Captain of the Bronx Homicide Division. He is the author of the book, "*Practical Homicide Investigations*" which has become the bible of investigative procedures for many police agencies across the nation. He has consulted in many of the nation's high profile murder cases and has conducted thousands of investigations. He is recognized worldwide as an expert in death investigations.

"*Blood Spatter Interpretation*" by Rod Englert.

Mr. Englert is a recognized expert in the field of blood spatter and pattern interpretation. His expertise was used in the O.J. Simpson case, as well as other high profile cases across the nation. He is one of the leading experts in the interpretation of blood left at the scene of a murder. By understanding some of the basic physics involved, one can tell a great deal about what occurred just by the pattern of the blood. For instance, blood at the scene can be in the form of a pool, which would indicate that the victim bled a great deal at that particular place (i.e., a victim falls to the floor from a fatal would, then the blood will pool around/under the victim at the location of the wound.) Blood can be left at the scene in the form of droplets, spatter, spray, and mist. Droplets are usually indicative of falling straight down and are easily recognizable. This can sometimes be a trail from the location where the injury occurred to the location of the body, or perhaps a trail from the location where the injury occurred to the point of exit, that is, where the victim or assailant left the area.

Spatter is the result of blood being cast outward with some degree of velocity. These patterns may be found on the walls, ceilings, furniture, and the floor. Spatter patterns are very important and should be scrutinized carefully. They can tell the investigator from which direction the blood came from. If blood hits an object at an angle, it will leave a "tail" behind it, much like that of a comet. "Cast off" is another form of spatter that leaves a different, but just as distinctive a pattern (i.e., blood on the ceiling has told investigators that the assailant made multiple strikes with the weapon.) In one particular case described by Mr. Englert, the assailant struck the victim with a blunt object several times. As he brought the weapon up for another strike, blood was cast off the weapon onto the ceiling. Investigators were able to reconstruct the scene to show that the victim had been bludgeoned to death. They were also able to place the assailant in the exact position he was standing when the assault occurred. The "tail" on a cast off is much longer and the line is often broken in several places. There are spray patterns, usually found when the blood follows the exit of a projectile, such as a bullet. Careful study of the spray pattern can assist in determining the location, height, and distance the victim was from the location of the spray.

I attended classes on interrogation/interviewing techniques taught by the John Reid School of Interviewing. This school is known worldwide and is considered the premier of interviewing schools. Through a series of pre-determined questions, and the close attention to the body language of the suspect, deception is easily detected. Key questions are used that are intended to elicit physiological responses that are indicative of truthfulness or deception. Humans exhibit specific behavioral characteristics when under stress. Knowledge and understanding of these behavioral patterns, when observed during the interview process, can give the interviewer the answers, even though the suspect may not verbalize a response.

I attended similar classes hosted by the Federal Bureau of Investigations and the Washington State Criminal Justice Training Commission. I invested numerous hours in classes that taught crime scene preservation, photography, scene interpretation, and evidence collection. But most beneficial of all was the hands-on experience that I got during the death investigations that I either conducted or participated in. I obtained valuable experience during each death investigation that cannot be obtained through any other process.

From Performance Evaluation.

.........Statistics of report ratio, clearance ratios and arrest ratio are all on the high end of Department normal. His reports are well written, [sic] showing good investigation/knowledge..............Jerry has followed through and done a very good job.
Sergeant D. Withrow

5

CHANCE TO PROVE

BY THE TIME I finally was assigned to the Detective Division, I had worked a lot of suicides and natural deaths, but wanted the chance to investigate an actual murder. I had seen the results of some of the death investigations conducted by the Department, and frankly was disappointed in the tactics and lack of results. I always thought that better investigations could be performed, and I wanted a chance to prove it to myself. I never learned to accept a death investigation as "routine," nor did I ever learn to leave them at work at the end of the day. Although it may have been a factor in solving cases, it would cause me a lot of sleepless nights. I would lay awake at night, my mind running like an endless video. I would create scenario after scenario, trying to replay how the crime might have occurred, based on the information and evidence I had. As each scenario played out, I would either discard it or keep the most plausible. Sometimes I would be drifting off to a fitful sleep, when an answer to a troubling question would pop into my head. Maybe it was something as simple as remembering an item or issue that I had forgotten to address that day. Sometimes it might be the answer as how to verify a statement made by someone.

The plausible ones, I would concentrate on as a piece of evidence, fitting it into place like a huge puzzle, one piece at a time. The picture would become clearer as each piece fit and was collaborated with either witness statements or other pieces of evidence. It seemed that with every piece that fit, there were hundreds that didn't.

Usually suspects are developed early on in an investigation, and it always made it easier to create the scenarios when there was a known suspect to place in it.

I would get up the following morning, still thinking about the investigation and I would start planning my day, based on the scenarios I had reviewed throughout the night.

6
THE DETECTIVE DIVISION

THE DETECTIVE SERGEANT was a 20+ year veteran of the Department and led the Detective Division at the Lewis County Sheriff's Office. He and I hit it off from the start and immediately became friends. He had a great personality and was easy to get along with. He would later be my Best Man when Susan and I got married in 1999. My friendship with him was never based on a professional mentorship because I didn't always agree with his investigative techniques.

He was a short, stalwart individual with a laid-back kind of personality. He wore thick rimmed glasses, had short brownish hair, a portly belly, and a thick neck. He had a constant red complexion that always reminded me of someone who was about to explode. It seemed that his favorite duties were leading the Crime Stoppers Program, and working boat patrol. Crime Stoppers kept him out of the office a great deal of the time; time that I personally thought could have been better utilized by being more actively involved in case investigations and the supervision of the Detectives, but that was not my call and the Crime Stoppers Program is a valuable tool. The boat patrols gave him overtime in the summer and let's face it, riding around in a boat or personal watercraft during summer isn't exactly rough duty. I always thought it was just one more thing to keep him away from what should have been his priority, the Detective Division.

He didn't respond to that many crime scenes in person, and often didn't take an active role in supervising major investigations. When he did arrive on a scene, he would make a few preliminary assignments, volunteer some observations and explanation, and then leave.

But before he left a scene, he always made sure that he reminded us to "watch the overtime."

Even though I liked him, I didn't always agree with his methods. In reality, murder investigations can't be set to a schedule if solving the crime is a priority. Leads have to be followed up when they are obtained and still "hot". If this means working all night, then that is what has to be done. Every day that goes by means clues and leads get colder and the perpetrator has more time to destroy evidence, create alibis, and witnesses have time to disappear.

From what I could see, everything was spontaneous with the Detective Division; they never appeared to have a plan for anything. Every death investigation and crime scene was approached as if it were their first one. I never saw any two homicides investigated the same way. Sure there were things that were similar, such as collecting evidence and interviewing witnesses, but the similarity stopped there. Some murder investigations involved canvassing the area and interviewing everyone in the vicinity, and some didn't. Some involved crime scene preservation, some didn't (the Amanda Reise case is an example). Some involved roadblocks in order to field interview every person who drove by the scene for the first 24 hours, some didn't. In one particular murder investigation (Betty Smith murder) that was being lead by one of the other Detectives, the roadblock method was done two weeks after the night of the murder! Needless to say, he never solved the crime. However, a hand-picked task force did solve the murder two years later; we did it within three weeks using the same information that had been available to the original Detective in charge two years before. Training teaches us that perpetrators will often drive by the scene within 24 hours to see what the police are doing. Being there to compile a list of names, addresses and identifying information will provide the investigators with a preliminary list to work from. Every name on the list is thoroughly investigated to determine if any had connections with the victim.

All major violent crimes in the county are investigated by the Sheriff's Office. One would just naturally assume that any agency with that kind of responsibility would certainly have a well trained, experienced Detective Division. The Sheriff's Office is the backbone of major crime investigations in the county and sadly, as far as I could tell, appeared to be the worst run, the least trained, and the worst equipped of all the Divisions.

It wouldn't be fair to leave it here, with just the Detectives taking all the blame. The Sheriff and his administration are responsible for not taking steps to make the necessary adjustments to improve areas of deficiency. My opinion is that the Sheriff was incompetent because he never seemed to address the real issues that ultimately could affect every citizen within his jurisdiction; shortage of patrol deputies, outdated equipment, and inept investigations, were just a few of the issues.

Even though some of the small towns like Morton, Mossyrock, Toledo, Winlock, and Napavine, have their own Police Departments, the Sheriff's Office still oversees all major crimes. This is just one more reason that any Sheriff and his top three deputies should take more responsibility in assuring the citizens have the best trained and most experienced homicide investigators the Department can provide. It seems to me that this has never been a priority for the Sheriff's Office in Lewis County. I once heard the Detective Sergeant say, "there aren't that many murders annually," therefore, they couldn't warrant a full-time homicide Detective. How many people have to be murdered in a one year period before the citizens deserve expert investigations? Every citizen of Lewis County should review the death investigations that have been conducted by the Lewis County Sheriff's Office for the past 20 years. Nothing will bring more meaning to the phrase "travesty of justice" than incomplete investigations.

During the five years I was a Detective, I attempted to establish a systematic and organized method to investigations. I was never completely successful because not only did it seem that I had to deal with resistance from my Sergeant, but the lack of concern of the Sheriff and his administration, as well. The apathy was so apparent at the Sheriff's Office that a Centralia Detective noted it in a letter she wrote. (See Amanda Reiss case)

There was only one other veteran Detective still remaining in the Detective Division that had been around as long as the Sergeant. Steve Wilson (name changed) had started his career with the Department after his tour in the military. He is truly one of the few people I know who seemed able to leave his work at the office at the end of the day. I never saw him get excited or deeply interested in any particular case, and assuming if he did, he was able to conceal it very well. There would be times that I would almost wish I could do the same.

Steve was the Department pilot and I never passed up a chance to go up with him. He flew over the mountains in the summer months looking for marijuana grows. It had become popular for growers to hide their outdoor grows in the forest. But they didn't realize that marijuana plants have a very distinct color and stand out like a sore thumb. Steve could spot a single marijuana plant from 2000 feet amongst the forest green of the Northwest. He taught me much about flying a plane and I always thought he would have been a great flight instructor. I never agreed with his investigative techniques, but like the Sergeant, he was my friend and was a Groomsman when Susan and I got married. In fact his father, who is a Minister, performed the services.

7

THE CONSEQUENCES

WHAT HAPPENS WHEN law enforcement refuses to change or correct its own insufficiencies? What happens to the justice system when citizens elect ego-maniacal individuals to positions of power? What happens when any agency's leaders place their own political agenda above the duties and responsibilities of their elected offices? What happens when officers are thrust into positions of investigator and have little or no training and skills for solving crimes? What are the consequences when agencies incorporate a "Rotational Detective Program?" I found some answers to those questions, and they are as upsetting as they are hard to believe. The answers I found came from only one agency, but I have to wonder how many more exist across the nation.

Society expects law enforcement to be proficient and at least a little smarter than the average criminal. Society pays for the services of law enforcement with the expectation that they are trained, educated, and proficient in solving crimes. When they are not, the results can be detrimental to the safety and security of our communities. They can undermine the trust of society in general. Families who have to endure the results of botched investigations become victims of the very system they depend on. Not only are the victims' families cheated out of justice, but society is cheated, as well, when perpetrators are left free to possibly strike again. The justice system is denied the opportunity to function as it was intended and murderers are allowed to walk free, sometimes to kill again. The lack of leadership and the presence of apathy in any law enforcement administration undermine the faith and trust in our law enforcement communities. When an agency allows ineptness to be repeated over and over, then I believe that agency and its administrators are no better than the criminals they fail to bring to justice.

The following stories are based on actual cases within the jurisdiction of a County Sheriff's Office in Washington State. Some of the stories may be hard to believe, but they are true and can be verified by their own respective case files. It is my opinion, based on time and exposure, that they are a product and result of two major factors in investigations; one is the "Rotational Detective Program" and the other is a Sheriff's administration who failed to recognize a pattern of poor investigations. Worse than failing to recognize the problem in my opinion, was their apparent lack of courage, concern, and willingness to correct it.

The "Rotational Detective Program" may seem like a good idea, if taken at face value. Proponents of the program say that it will provide for a better-trained Department in that eventually more of the officers in the field will have investigative experience. It allows for some type of temporary advancement of individual officers in agencies that otherwise have few opportunities for deputies to try something different. After a two or three year assignment, the officer goes back to patrol deputy status and a new officer is assigned to take the place of the officer rotating out. Sounds reasonable so far, right?

The rotational program provides an opportunity for an officer to experience a change of pace, at the same time learn new things. However, in reality, it is rare if any of the other proposed purposes ever occur. The training an officer receives in a short stint as a Detective is minimal and of little use when that officer is back on patrol. The officer is not going to be conducting the homicide investigation; the new rotational Detective will be. The claims made by the proponents of the rotational program become even less credible when the results fall short of what should be expected of a professional investigative Division. The problem is compounded when the jurisdiction of the law enforcement agency does not experience a high volume of homicides. It takes years of training and countless hours of exposure to death scenes to become proficient in investigating homicides. There are many facets of homicide investigations; each one is an expertise in itself. Photography, evidence collection, forensic technologies, the ability and knowledge to utilize that technology, blood spatter interpretation, interviewing/interrogation skills, and even some knowledge of human anatomy are all necessary skills. In many cases, the investigator has to attend the autopsies and be able to recognize the damage caused by a fatal injury. It is usually the investigator in the smaller agencies that will take the photographs during the autopsy process and collect the evidence. Then, if the case goes to trial, the investigator will often have to give testimony to the findings and results that were observed during the autopsy.

How do you think it would be perceived by a jury if the lead Detective couldn't answer a question about post-mortem lividity, fixed lividity, rigor mortis or petechial hemorrhaging? These are just a few of the things that have to be learned and understood by a good investigator. From profiling a suspect, to analytically evaluating a crime scene, the expertise required to solve murder cases simply does not occur in a rotational program. There is just not enough time, training, or actual hands-on exposure to create any expertise. The end result is that citizens are being denied professional homicide investigations. How would you feel if you found out that the "lead investigator" of a murdered family member had never had any formal homicide investigative training, had never investigated a murder, and had just come off the road working traffic? It has happened too many times, and it still continues. Not only did the Lewis County Sheriff's Office practice the Rotational Detective Program, but shortly after I quit in 2001, they assigned a Patrol Sergeant as the acting Detective Sergeant. In 2004, a second Patrol Sergeant was given his turn as leader of the Detective Division. Neither of these Patrol Sergeants were investigators. As of May 2008, the Detective Division is being headed up by a rookie Sergeant who's only extensive investigative expertise lies in child sex crime investigations. So, the citizens not only have been denied expert Detectives, but are being denied expert leadership in the Detective Division as well. I have a strong belief that you cannot create a new program with old talent! It is my opinion that is why the Lewis Count Sheriff's Office still remains far behind other agencies in leadership, equipment, skill and properly trained personnel.

The following cases are a testimony to what I believe to be inept and amateur attempts by Detectives who were faced with investigations that were beyond their abilities to investigate. One source stated it best when he said, "The results are an embarrassment to anyone who commits their life to serving humanity by taking on the gruesome task of death investigations."

As far as I am concerned, the methods and techniques used in most of the investigations in this book are more suited to the attics of the Keystone Cops. The only thing missing is the silence of the still films; that and the elected Coroner who never responded to a death scene that I participated in during the 12 years I was there.

This program is unfair to the deputies who are suddenly given the title of Detective and the responsibilities of investigations when the day before they were writing traffic tickets and answering barking dog complaints! What is wrong with an agency that allows this and places such huge responsibilities on those who are doing the best they can under the circumstances?

These are questions that every citizen in the nation should be demanding their elected official's respond to.

8

Mossyrock Murder

THE FIRST EXPERIENCE I had with the Lewis County Sheriff's Office's investigative techniques and abilities occurred while I was Chief of Police in Mossyrock. In 1990, three male individuals were drinking in the lounge at the Fireside Inn. This restaurant and lounge was located at the intersection of U.S. State Route 12 and Williams St. in Mossyrock. It was a favorite stopover for hunters and fisherman. On this particular night in question, three men from Tacoma had been fishing in the area and had stopped in for a few beers before going home.

I found out through local gossip the following morning that a man had been shot at the Fireside Inn during the night. I contacted the business owner and she told me the following: Three men had been in the lounge drinking and two of them had gotten into an argument. They eventually went out to their pick up truck that was parked on the north side of the building. Patrons could see them from inside the lounge. The three men appeared to still be arguing and all three got into the truck. There was some scuffling and then a gunshot was heard. The men then proceeded to drive away. I then contacted the Sheriff's office and was told that they were investigating the shooting and they told me the following: Apparently two of the men had driven to the Tacoma Police Department the morning after the shooting and contacted the police. They had arrived in the pickup, and in the back was the body of the third man. The story they told was that there had been an accidental discharge of a handgun in the cab of the truck and their friend had been shot. They drove about 1/4 mile west of the restaurant and pulled him out of the truck, laying him on the side of the highway. They claimed to have attempted CPR and when that failed, they put the body in the bed of the truck and drove home to Tacoma. After sleeping the night, they decided to go to the police.

I was a little upset that the Sheriff's Office had started the investigation without contacting me when they first learned of the shooting. It is common courtesy to let the primary jurisdiction know when an investigation is starting by the county Sheriff's Office. By normal standards and procedures I would have been asked to participate since it occurred in Mossyrock.

For the next several weeks I tried to do what I could to assist in the investigation by way of talking to the locals who had been in the bar the night of the shooting. I might have been new at law enforcement, but I had enough common sense to know that this was a very suspicious shooting. What I didn't understand was the way the Detectives at the Sheriff's Office operated as though I didn't exist. There were no attempts by them to include me in any briefings or discussions, not even an overture of professional courtesy at any time.

Every day for the next few months, I would expect to pick up the local paper and read about an arrest being made in the shooting incident. The arrests never came and the investigation quietly faded into an abyss, along with other investigated homicides.

It wasn't until I was working for the Sheriff's Office several years later that I discovered just how bad the Sheriff's Office's investigation really had been. It was while I was reviewing the case file time that I learned more about the investigation. I had made a practice of pulling old cases and reviewing them, just in case there was a chance they could be resurrected. Sometimes a fresh look at an old investigation by someone else will provide insight and a different perspective. Sometimes something so small and seemingly insignificant can be overlooked the first time around.

I never considered myself an expert at the time, but I had a deep burning desire to do everything I could to solve murders. There is something about a murderer walking free that incites a personal duty in me to bring them to justice. The idea of some "worthless low-life" killing another human being and, worse yet, getting away with it, is not something I will ever accept. My Sergeant often told me that I needed to "let some of the investigations go, that some were going to fall through the cracks". I told him that I refused to start an investigation with that kind of mindset. It was self-defeating and it took away from the motivation to solve the case.

Now let us review the Mossyrock shooting again, based on what I had learned on my own during the time of the incident, plus adding the information I obtained from the original reports.

When I interviewed the witnesses right after the shooting, this is what they told me: That the three men had been in the bar drinking and had mentioned that they had been fishing at Swofford Pond. Two of the men had gotten into an argument after a few beers and then decided to leave. The three of them went out to their Ford pickup truck; an early 60's model. Witnesses inside the lounge watched as one of the men who were arguing got into the truck from the passenger side and slid over to the center, while his partner got in from the passenger side. The other male who had been arguing was standing with the driver's door open and appeared to be arguing again with the man sitting in the center. A gunshot was heard and the men then quickly left the parking lot.

The Story

The story the men told law enforcement was that when they left the lounge, the man in the center and the man on the passenger side were looking at a hand gun. The passenger said he was passing the gun back and forth and it accidentally went off, striking the victim, entering from the right side. Both men stated that they pulled to the side of the road and placed the victim on the ground so they could administer CPR. After an unsuccessful attempt, and the determination that their friend was dead, they loaded him into the back of the truck and drove home; their home being in Tacoma, which was about 80 miles away. They said they each went to their own home and went to bed. The next morning they got together and discussed the shooting. Then they decided to drive to the police station where they reported the incident.

Both men were given polygraph tests and both failed. The investigation stopped and the case went on the shelf. What's wrong with this picture, folks?

Let's take a look at the evidence. The autopsy revealed that the bullet entered from the left side, traveling at an upward angle. (Remember the passenger said it entered the right side.) The blood spatter inside the truck showed that the bullet exited the right side of the victim, causing a large amount of spray throughout the passenger side of the truck. This was consistent with what the witnesses at the lounge saw and heard. The path of travel of the bullet was consistent with the gun being fired from the driver's side. There was no indication or mention in any of the reports of any powder burns on the victim, thus eliminating the possibility of a contact or close contact wound. This added to the evidence that the gun had been fired from a distance of at least two feet or more. The two friends made no attempt to get their friend to a hospital. They went home and slept that night; the body left outside in the back of the truck.

My thoughts were that the men went home and spent the night fabricating their alibi. Once they were comfortable with their story, and with each other sticking to it, they then went to the police station.

Much to my dismay, none of the reports that I had sent to the Sheriff's Office were in the case file. I asked the Detective Sergeant about the missing reports and he said he had never received them. He could not remember having seen them. He agreed to have the case reviewed by the prosecutor again. The prosecutor said that it could have been prosecuted at the time it occurred, but the statue of limitation had run out on a manslaughter charge. Apparently they never considered a murder charge. So much time had gone by it seemed it may very well be impossible to make a case. To make matters worse, the truck that had been used during the shooting had been placed in an outside storage area. The area is fenced by an eight foot high chain-link fence with the west end being the wall of a three story apartment building. The exposure to the elements, as well as the garbage dumped out of the windows of the old apartments, had completely contaminated what evidence there was. Any evidence removed from the truck at this stage would have been easily suppressed by a good defense attorney. That is, there is no way the Sheriff's Office can say that it would have been impossible for someone to have entered the storage area and tampered with the truck. Anyone desiring to gain access to the storage area could do so by climbing over the fence or accessing it from one of the apartment windows. Every time I was confronted with something like this, I just shook my head in amazement at the lack of professionalism and concern the Sheriff's Office displayed.

Even with all this I felt we had to try. I read and re-read the case file along with attempting to recall everything I could from the part

I'd had in the original investigation. I finally located a phone number for the girlfriend of the shooter. I struggled with the decision of whether to call her or not. I knew there was only going to be one chance at this and there would never be another chance to get the truth out. I finally made the phone call to her. I identified myself and told her that the case had been reopened. I tried to sound a lot more confident than I felt. My hope was that I could get her to give up her boyfriend. I tried to convince the shooter's girlfriend that an arrest was imminent and that she should not put herself in a position of being a co-conspirator. But, it was not to be, and they'd had several years to become entrenched in their alibi. Today, there are two more murderers walking free.

9

MISSING PERSON

IN 1983, A local female disappeared without a trace. Donna Jean was 53 years old at the time. At 5 foot 2 inches and 130 lbs, she was full of energy. Her shoulder length brown hair was always neatly combed and she was most comfortable in jeans and tennis shoes. She especially enjoyed her granddaughter, and spent as much time with her as possible. She loved wearing the pink and white tennis shoes that her granddaughter had given her as a birthday gift. Donna Jean had been born and raised in Lewis County, and she loved the area she lived in. Her parents had homesteaded and built the house she had been born in, and she never lost her love for the old place. It was one of her favorite places to go to when she wanted solitude, or just to visit and reminisce. It had long been vacant and stood hidden from view from the road behind a cover of Douglas Firs and Hemlock trees and for many years a locked gate kept visitors out.

The Lewis County Sheriff's Office conducted the investigation, as it does with all major crimes within Lewis County. Apparently the investigation was exhausted after a few months and the case went into what I call the "county abyss." This abyss is full of unsolved cases ranging from thefts, robberies and assaults, to the most heinous double murder.

The disappearance of the local female occurred before I made the career change to law enforcement. But, I knew her family and remembered the event through the news media and discussions in the community. I remembered the extensive news coverage for a short period of time by the local paper and, like many other cases, it quietly faded away from the public. In a very short time, it was forgotten by the majority of the community, but certainly never forgotten by her family.

Thirteen years later, in the summer of 1996, I was in my unmarked vehicle heading to a residence to conduct an interview. It was a beautiful day and I was enjoying being out of the office. But the peacefulness was suddenly broken by the ringing of my car phone. It was my Sergeant on the phone and he instructed me to meet him at one of the private estates just outside one of the small communities; on State Route 12 East of I-5. This area consists of a few small businesses, a volunteer Fire Department and a tavern. There are the usual small number of residences that accompany these typical rural communities. The estate sits on a hill and is about 1 1/2 miles from where Donna Jean lived in 1983.

I arrived at the estate and drove up the long drive with its immaculate fences and manicured lawns on both sides. The beautifully landscaped home was to my right and I could see the Sergeant's station wagon parked about a hundred yards off to my left, near an old house. As I drove up to his location and got out of the car, I saw an off duty Washington State Trooper I knew. Greg Link was in civilian work clothes and dirty enough for me to know that he must have been tearing the old farm house down. Most of the roof had been removed, and there were various stacks of lumber that had been cleaned and sorted.

He told us that he had been in the process of removing the last section of the roof at the south west corner of the old house. As he tore through the shingles he could see what appeared to be skeletal remains of something lying between the 2x6 ceiling joists. He got down into the attic area for a closer look and realized they were the skeletal remains of a human partially wrapped in clear plastic. He also noted that there were some items of clothing with the bones and at least one pink and white tennis shoe. He thought he had been able to identify the remnants of a bra and with the color of the shoe being pink he offered the possibility of it being a female. At least with him being in law enforcement he knew enough to back out of what at the moment became a crime scene. That is, the moment the skeletal remains were found, the immediate area became a crime scene and had to be treated as one. The remains had obviously been there for a very long time and a great deal of disturbance had occurred due to the dismantling of the building. But it was, for all practical purposes, a crime scene. This was a concept I was never able to get the Detective Division and Administration to adopt, even though it is one of the basic fundamentals of investigations.

My Sergeant made his one and only accurate observation when he suggested that it might be the missing female from 13 years earlier. He had been involved in the original investigation into her disappearance in 1983. He was able to provide me with a little history about the investigation. He knew that the old farm house where the remains were found had been the original homestead of the missing women's parents. He was able to recall that the house had been searched by members of the Search and Rescue Unit within days after she had disappeared, and nothing had been found. He even recalled that someone had suggested the possibility of a mountain lion dragging her away from her residence.

I remember thinking when he told me this that it fit with the pattern I was becoming familiar with. If they couldn't come to a logical conclusion, then they would offer some far fetched possibility that made no sense at all, and was absent of any supporting evidence.

I started to take photographs from the ground, in no hurry to climb the ladder to the attic. This was not due to any reluctance to get to the remains, but simply that it helps to take the time to look around and let your thoughts flow freely, trying to get a feel for the area, the scene, and mentally getting to the right place. After all, if this was the missing female, then a lot of evidence had disappeared after thirteen years and we were not going to get a second chance if we missed anything. But my Sergeant was already calling for the Coroner and getting paper bags out of his car. I had planned on spending some time on the ground taking photographs and getting a plan formulated as to how I wanted to proceed. My Sergeant was heading up the ladder before I finished my first roll of film, and I knew that if I wanted to see things in their original position, I had better get up there with him. At the top of the ladder I looked back toward the rear of the attic. The roof shingles had been removed almost to the end so there was plenty of light and, for once, it wasn't raining. In the center of the attic, located about four feet from the end, was a brick chimney. There were numerous articles of trash, old newspapers and cardboard boxes throughout the attic area. We are only talking about an area approximately sixteen feet wide and 24 feet long. Originally there had been a wall on the East end where the ladder was. A door about two feet by four feet gave access to the attic. I collected as much of the cardboard and paper as seemed reasonable to have tested for latent prints later.

Removing the Remains

As we worked our way back to the remains, it was evident that 13 years worth of exposure to the small animals and birds had resulted in bones being torn apart, and some had been carried away. There were several old bottles, pieces of plastic, and papers between the ceiling joists, along with the scattered remains. There were, however, enough of the remains intact to get a clear picture of how the body position would have been in 1983. There was an old eight ounce drinking glass several feet from the remains and an empty aspirin bottle about two feet from the glass. As soon as my Sergeant saw these he offered the possibility that she had committed suicide by overdosing on aspirin. I reminded him that the remains were partially wrapped in plastic and most likely had been completely wrapped at one time. He suggested that since she was a woman, and "they didn't like dirt," she had brought the plastic with her to lie on. I thought, "Yeah, and they don't like dark, scary places like attics either." He didn't stick around long after that and I was left to finish up. He even released the building back to the owner, telling him we wouldn't be back for any additional work.

While I waited for the Deputy Coroner, I kept studying the skeleton. I noticed that the skull was up against the shingles at the eave block. There was a nail protruding through the shingles and touching the skull. I wondered how comfortable that could have been for her if she had pushed herself that tight into the roof while waiting to die. I also found directly under what would have been her back, was an electrical outlet box for a ceiling light. At this point I knew the Sergeant's suicide theory was less plausible then it was when he first rendered it. I couldn't believe that anyone was going to climb into an attic, wrap themselves in plastic, lie between ceiling joists, push themselves so tight into the roof to be poked with a nail, and just lie there until they died. Not to mention lying on top of an electrical outlet box. Sometimes just plain old common sense will go along way. And, it's not always suicide.

One piece of clothing stood out more than the other items. It was a blue denim coat which looked rather large for a small female. It looked to be in better condition than that of most of the other items of clothing, and at the time I had no idea how significant that coat would be.

I spent a considerable amount of time just sitting and looking at the remains. The skull and disconnected bones, mixed with items of clothing were all that were left of what was once a living, breathing human being. I wondered what her last thoughts were. How did she die? I stared at the skull and could almost feel the spirit of this once living person pleading with me to bring justice so she could finally rest in peace. This would end up being how it was with all future death investigations for me. I would feel a connection with the deceased victim, being their last friend who was the eternal link between them, their families, and the truth about their death.

When the Deputy Coroner arrived, we tried to pick everything up and keep it all in the plastic. This meant dirt, trash and all the clothing remained together in the body bag. I wanted as much evidence as possible to sort through at the Coroner's Office. This way I would be assured a clean working area and the time to sort through everything in a thorough manner. As we were picking up the smaller scattered pieces of bone, I found a denture plate near the tennis shoe. This would be vital in obtaining positive identification through dental records.

After the remains were loaded in the Coroner's vehicle and the Deputy Coroner drove away, I went back through the scene one last time. There was nothing left to do now but wait until the Pathologist examined the bones for signs of injuries. We had, at least, a place to start. We had an unsolved disappearance of a female thirteen years prior and we now had skeletal remains that had obviously been decomposing for a very long time.

The next day I went to the Coroner's facility and began the job of separating the clothing from the bag of bones and debris. Each piece of clothing was carefully spread out on brown wrapping paper. I examined each item with a magnifying glass. I was looking for anything that might have been a blood stain, hair, or damage that may have been caused by a knife or a gunshot. With considerable damage already done by rats, mice, insects and birds, it was very difficult to determine if there had been a knife or gunshot through them. As

Jerry C. Berry | WHERE MURDERERS WALK FREE

each piece of clothing was examined, I placed it into its own bag. The next process involved removing all the bones and placing them on the stainless steel table. Every bone and bone fragment was examined by the Pathologist. A great deal of attention was given to the ribs, vertebrae and skull. These would be the most likely to produce evidence of a knife or gunshot injury. Every scrape we found on the bones were carefully examined to determine if they could have been caused by an injury or were just the gnawing marks of some small animal. The final conclusion was that no evidence of trauma to the skull or bones was found. But remember, this did not mean that a knife or bullet could not have passed through the body without striking bone. What it did mean was that the manner of death would not be easy to determine.

The next day, I called Dr. Ray, the King County Medical Examiner. I wanted to know about the possibility of an overdose on Aspirin. I had to consider the Sergeant's theory on the "suicide by aspirin". I had always been willing to consider every possibility and suggestion, regardless how ridiculous I personally thought it was. Every possibility has to be either substantiated or refuted. Dr. Ray told me that it would take a large quantity of Aspirin to cause death, and the death would be a slow and painful one. He explained that just prior to expiring; the subject would go into convulsions, thrashing around in immense pain. To me, this ruled out the suicide theory. If I were to believe Dr Ray, the victim would not have been found in the position she was and certainly would not have remained wrapped in the plastic.

I contacted the daughter of the victim, and told her we had found the remains of an unidentified person. When I told her where it had been found, she started crying and told me that was one of her mother's favorite places. It had been in her mother's family for a long time and her mother had been born there. She asked if we had found pink and white tennis shoes. She said her daughter, had bought the shoes not long before her mother disappeared. I told her we had found a shoe like that and she asked if they were Nikes. I didn't know at that time what brand they were and I told her I didn't know. I made arrangements for her and her daughter to come in and look at the clothing, to see if she could identify any of them.

The following day I had the evidence laid out in a neat fashion, so the two ladies could see them. When the daughter and granddaughter arrived, I led them into the room and stood off to one side as they looked at each item. They were able to identify the shoes and a leopard colored scarf as belonging to Donna Jean. The blue denim jacket with the big lower front pockets was one item that neither of them recognized. They both were adamant that the coat did not belong to the victim.

This was a very difficult time for them and I wondered how it felt to be identifying the remains of a loved one after thirteen years. What goes on in a person's mind when they are looking at items that they know belonged to their missing loved one? My heart ached for them, and in these situations I was always left with the feeling that no matter what we did, it would never be enough.

I still had not received the results from the forensic orthodontist for dental identification, but watching the two ladies I already knew that Donna Jean had finally been found.

After they left, I went to the Records Section and pulled the original case file from 1983. I spent several days going through the file over and over, looking for anything that might point to a possible suspect. I found one I considered to be the most likely. He was one of the victim's former boyfriends. He had been a suspect during the original investigation along with several others. The problem that I saw in the original investigation was that no one seemed to focus on a definitive suspect and work it to a successful conclusion. They would bounce back and forth from one suspect to another, plus throw in the "theories" about mountain lions and possible abduction by a passing truck. The passing truck theory was based on an erroneous report that a truck "had been heard on State Route 12, near the victim's house" in the early hours of the morning she was found missing. I thought to myself, this is the Northwest where there are hundreds of log trucks and chip trucks running up and down State Route 12, 24 hours a day, 7 days a week. You think it was unusual to hear a truck there"? Give me a break! The theories had no foundation and only disrupted any focus on a viable suspect. I realized that the investigative practices of the Lewis County Sheriff's Office hadn't changed much, if at all, over the years. It is my opinion that the common denominators were, and still are, a lack of training and skill.

I spent a great deal of time talking to the victim's daughter and granddaughter, trying to learn as much about Donna Jean's history, lifestyle and daily habits, as possible. I learned that she had a routine that she followed every night when she was home. Just before she went to bed, she would turn down the blankets and turn on the light on the stand next to her bed. She would place her eye glasses on the nightstand, then go out to the back yard and carry in enough firewood to get through the night. She always kept a pair of gloves that she used just for the purpose of carrying in the wood. These were kept near the wood box near the stove. She would then secure the doors and go to bed. I learned that she was having some problems with a former boyfriend. She had broken off her relationship with him and he had begun to harass her. He had initiated a civil suit against her, trying to recover money that he thought she owed him. He had been questioned during the original investigation and had even taken a polygraph. The little bit of information they had at the time should have made him a primary suspect and main focus of the original investigation.

Finally, it was time to consider a press release. There are two ways to handle press releases during a homicide investigation. One is to draw as much public attention to the case as possible, and the other is to keep it away from the public until the appropriate time. Each one has a unique advantage, but with each one, timing is crucial. If investigators have critical information known only to them and the perpetrator, and the perpetrator is known, then that information should be kept from the media. You never want to alert the perpetrator that you have information that might lead to him. In the case of this victim, we had a thirteen year old case and no solid leads or evidence. I decided to get the story out to the public as soon as possible and with as much detail as possible. Either way there is a certain element of risk, but sometimes you have to choose what you think is the best and just maybe, someone will read the paper and remember something from 1983.

I contacted a reporter from the local newspaper and provided him with as much information as was necessary without suggesting we had no leads. When the article came out, it was front page news and included photos of the victim. Within 24 hours the break I had prayed for came through. I received a call from a male who said that he may know who killed her. This person who I will call "Fred," (not his real name) told me that he thought his uncle had killed her. He said he remembered being in the living room of his parent's house in 1983 with his father, his uncle, and his father's best friend. His father's best friend had been very angry with Donna Jean and was expressing his anger when he made the comment, "I wish she was dead." Fred said that he remembered thinking at the time, "Boy, you have no idea who you just said that in front of," referring to his uncle. Fred said that his uncle had always been crazy and that he would do anything. A few days after this conversation took place, Donna Jean disappeared. Fred said his uncle soon left the area and he always suspected that his uncle and his fathers' best friend had been responsible for the victim's disappearance. He wanted to remain anonymous and I told him that I could do that for a while, but I was going to have to talk with his father and mother. I agreed to give him a couple of days to prepare his parents for my visit. Whether or not I would talk to them was not an option, it was going to happen. His uncle was his mother's brother, and apparently everyone in the family was terrified of him.

I waited two days and then called Fred's father, making arrangements to meet with him at his residence. When I arrived at Fred's parent's home, I was greeted by a friendly elderly gentleman in his early sixties. I introduced myself and was invited in. I will refer to Fred's father as "Don" and his mother as "Sarah." (not their real names) Don said that he did remember the conversation that Fred had told me about. He had not paid that much attention to it at the time and thought that his friend was just expressing his anger. He did say that his brother-in-law was probably capable of murder and would not have put it past him to have killed her. He told me that his brother-in-law had a friend with him the night the conversation took place and the guy's name was Jimmy Smith. He told me that he and his friend had spent a lot of time fishing on the Cowlitz River and that his friend's son had gone with them, on occasion. He told me that his friend's son was still in the area, as far as he knew. He denied that his friend had talked about the disappearance of the female, and denied having ever suspected his friend of being involved. Don told me that his wife was reluctant to talk to me because she was afraid that her brother would come back and kill her if he found out. I told him to tell his wife that I wanted to talk to her and to call me as soon as she was available. It may seem that I continue to refer to myself as the only investigator, but keep in mind I was given very little assistance with this investigation. Like so many other investigations in Lewis County, the Detectives are often on their own.

The next morning I got a call from Sarah, who agreed to meet me at her place of employment. At 2:00 pm, I arrived at Sarah's workplace and made my way through the crowd to the dining area where I was to meet Sarah. I asked the waitress for Sarah and she said she would get her for me. A few minutes later a middle aged woman came to my table and introduced herself as Sarah. She sat down and I began by asking her to tell me what she knew about the conversation that Fred had told me about. She said that she had not been present when the conversation took place, but had been told about it by her son Fred. She said that she knew her brother was capable of anything and that she was afraid that if he ever found out that she had talked to me, he would come back and kill her. She told me that in 1983 her brother had been hanging out with an older man named Jimmy Smith who was from the Tacoma area. She said Jimmy was a loser and she remembered him to be very "weird." She said that Jimmy had been staying with her brother in a single-wide mobile home near Onalaska, Washington. As she described the single-wide trailer and its location, I knew exactly where it was. I drove by it on a regular basis and it was one of several that had always been rental units.

She really had nothing to tell me specifically about Donna Jean's disappearance, but she certainly corroborated Don's and Fred's statements about her brother's capacity to commit murder, and the fact that her brother and the victim's boyfriend could be connected, as well as being in the area at the time of her disappearance.

I would spend the next few weeks going over the case file and talking with Donna Jean's daughter and granddaughter. It seemed as if I had the whole case file memorized; I had read it so many times. The daughter had even hired a physic who told her that her mother was buried in a shallow grave in a gravel pit not far from where she lived at the time. She had never quit trying to find her mother and she never believed the original investigation had been thorough enough. Having read the reports, and knowing that the old homestead place had been supposedly searched, I was inclined to agree with her. She told me that her mother's boyfriend had a son who worked at a restaurant in one of the nearby towns. He had always gotten along with the Donna Jean and apparently Donna Jean liked him. I decided that it was time to pay this guy a visit.

I contacted him at his residence. He was the only person so far who was willing to talk freely, and even volunteered to help in any way he could. He told me that he had always suspected his father had been responsible for Donna Jean's disappearance. He asked what I had found with the body and I told him about the items of clothing. When I mentioned the coat, he asked if it was a large denim coat with two big pockets in the front near the bottom. I felt an excitement run through my body and it was hard for me to control my response! I told him in as calm a manner as possible, that he had just described the coat. He said that his father had always worn a coat like that when they went fishing, and that it was his favorite. He even suggested I have it tested to see if there were any fish scales in the pockets. He said that his father carried fishing tackle in the big front pockets and there might be fish scales from past fishing trips.

He told me that his father had been very abusive to him, his sister, and his mother. His mother finally got a divorce and finished raising him and his sister on her own.

He thought that he could get his dad to admit he had killed the victim if he had the chance to talk to him. He thought that he might be able to at least get his dad to implicate himself. I had already found the location of Donna Jean's former boyfriend and even had a phone number for him. The son agreed to make a call to his father and allow me to tape record the conversation. I believed I had enough probable cause to obtain a search warrant, allowing me to intercept and record the conversation.

Washington State is a "two party consent" state, which basically means it takes the consent of both parties to have their conversation recorded. For this reason, a search warrant would be required in order for me to intercept and record the pending call from the son to his father without the suspect's knowledge. I spent almost two days writing and rewriting the search warrant before it was ready to present to the judge. I could write most search warrants in less than one hour, but this one had to be perfect. I didn't want to have a murder conviction overturned because of a poorly written search warrant.

I admit I was a little nervous when I entered the Judge's Chambers and presented the search warrant affidavit for him to read. This was the first wire tap or communication intercept search warrant I had ever done, and it was a stressful few minutes for me as I sat waiting for the Judge to read it. When he was done, he asked me to raise my right hand. At that point I knew the warrant was approved and I completed the process by swearing that everything in the affidavit was true. The judge affixed his signature and wished me good luck; I was past this hurdle.

I called the son and made arrangements for a time for him to make the call. When I arrived at his residence I busied myself setting up the recording equipment and making sure that the son knew the key questions to ask. There was only going to be one shot at this and there was no way to rehearse for it. We would start with a basic strategy and hope for the best. There was no way to predict what the father's reactions were going to be or what his responses were going to be.

After everything was hooked up, I went over the questions that I wanted him to ask; questions that I hoped would elicit some sort of confession or answers that would implicate him. After a few moments it was time to make the call. I took a deep breath and nodded to him, the signal to start dialing. I listened through the ear piece as the wheels on the recorder turned. One ring, two rings, three, four, five. Was the anxiety and stress of the moment for nothing? The jerk wasn't even home? Then suddenly a male voice on the other end said "hello." The connection had been made, and the next few minutes could very well bring to a close a thirteen year old case. I found myself holding my breath at times as the son talked, waiting anxiously for each response from the father. But no matter how he tried to convince his father that he knew the truth about Donna Jean's death, his father kept denying it. His denials had a sound of practiced and rehearsed consistency rather than the ring of truth, but he was not going to budge from his denial. The son had done a good job trying to convince his dad that "the cops" had evidence and he told his father about the coat. His father told him that he had "lost that coat" and didn't have any idea how it ended up with the body. After about 45 minutes the suspect hung up on his son, the only time during the call that the suspect showed any sign that his son was getting to him.

I left feeling defeated and knew that it was a major setback in my hopes of getting enough to get a murder warrant issued for the suspect. The suspect was now residing on the East coast and was retired. As I traveled back to my office in Chehalis, I decided I would contact the Police Department where the suspect lived and find out if they had any knowledge of him. If I ever did get enough information to obtain a murder warrant for him, I would certainly need the help of the local Police Department when it came time to make the arrest.

As soon as I got back to my office I made a call to the Police Department and spoke to the Lieutenant. After I explained what I was working on and who it involved, he told me he would do some checking and call me back. True to his word, the Lieutenant called back within the hour. He had more information than I had hoped for and after the failure with the recorded call, I needed a boost. The Lieutenant told me that the suspect had a history of domestic violence related contacts with his Department. It appeared that he had a girlfriend that he liked to push around. The girlfriend, an African-American middle-aged woman, recently broke off her relationship with him after he struck her and tried to force her out of her vehicle. He had been arrested at the time and apparently had never quit blaming her for his arrest. The Lieutenant gave me her name to talk to and described her as a very nice, but gutsy, lady.

Emily Harris (not her real name) was indeed a nice lady and turned out to be a great source of information to me. She told me that she no longer lived with the suspect, but did visit him on occasion. They had patched up their differences to a point that they apparently could keep a limited relationship going. I told Emily about the case and how I came to suspect her friend. She told me that she had always suspected there was something in his past that he kept to himself. She couldn't explain why she felt this way, but she did. She told me that she believed that he was capable of killing, and she would not be surprised at all if he had. She said she would be willing to do anything to help and wanted my number, saying she would call me if she came up with anything.

It had been over a month since the remains of the missing female had been found. I wouldn't release the remains to the family for burial and knew that it was bothering them. I explained to Donna Jean's family that it was very important for me to keep the remains accessible in case we needed it for further forensic testing. I told them that I had a few leads that may lead me to the killer. Once they heard this, they told me to keep the remains as long as I needed to. I didn't go into details about the direction the investigation was going, but they had a right to know a little. I never believed in keeping families of murdered victims in the dark. They were entitled to know how and if the case was being thoroughly investigated.

It was time to spend a few days going over the old case file again and to evaluate everything I had learned since the victim's remains had been found. I needed to get everything organized and some kind of plan formulated to proceed with. Based on the information in the original case file, and what I had learned since the remains had been found, I had the following:

On December 14, 1983, Donna Jean's granddaughter had spent the day with her. She had left her grandmother at her residence at about Noon, going back to her mother's residence. Witnesses verified that the victim had attended the evening service at the Community Church, which was about two blocks down the road. There are about a dozen houses between the church and the house the victim lived in. Witnesses verified that she had been in a good mood at the evening service, and had stood outside afterwards talking with a young couple with a new baby. She left the church at about 7:30 p.m., walking to her residence, which was about a five minute walk. The following morning, after several calls and no answers, the daughter went to her mother's residence and found the following: Donna Jean's eyeglasses were on the night stand next to her bed, the lamp was still on and the blankets were turned down with no obvious signs that the bed had been slept in, her purse was on the kitchen table where she usually left it, and nothing appeared to be missing. The gloves she used while carrying in wood were found on the swing set in the back yard and her car was in the drive and had not been tampered with.

When investigators arrived, they found shoe prints below one of the windows at the rear of the house. According to the reports, it looked as if someone had spent considerable time standing under the window. (There is no record or mention in the case file that any casts were taken of the shoe prints.) No evidence was found in the house, yard, or surrounding area. None of the neighbors contacted had seen the victim leave the residence. The backyard was bordered by large Fir trees and Alder trees, which allowed ample hiding places. A short distance behind the trees, the terrain changed to a gradual decline of about fifty feet into a small creek. Across the creek and up an incline through thick brush, an old logging road led a short distance to State Route 12.

We knew Donna Jean had taken her boyfriend to the old homestead on a few occasions. We knew she was fighting with her boyfriend and was involved in a civil suit with him. The old homestead had been searched, at least the original report stated as much. We knew the boyfriend, Fred's uncle, and the old man Jimmie had left the area a short time after she disappeared. We had a coat that had been found with the remains that had been described by the son as the type belonging to his father during that time period.

Trying to create a plausible scenario based on this information, I considered the following as a possibility: Her boyfriend would have been familiar with her habits and evening patterns. He would have known the area behind her house, as well as being familiar with the old homestead, which was secluded and behind a locked gate. He could have parked his car on the old logging road out of sight, walked up to the rear of her house, and watched her through the window. This would explain the shoe prints investigators found, but failed to cast. He may have made contact with her when she came out to the woodpile, rendered her helpless and carried her through the trees to his car. Her boyfriend was a large man over six feet and she was about five feet, one inch and weighed about 110 pounds. It would have been easy for him to have done this, and even more so if he had been assisted by Fred's uncle and the old man. It was then a short trip to the old homestead where they could have killed her, and then took the time needed to hide the body.

I believe that after the body had been deposited behind the chimney, the numerous cardboard boxes that we found had been stacked up on each side of the chimney. For anyone looking into the attic from the small entry door, it would have appeared that the boxes and chimney were at the very end of the building. This would have explained the negative results of the search of the old house. The plastic would have contained the odor for several weeks. Perhaps the killer had gotten blood on the coat and that was why it was left with the body. The fact that there was no flashlight found would indicate that she had not walked to that location during the night. There were no other suspects found who had as strong a motive as her boyfriend, and we know he had a propensity for violence.

The only thing to do was locate the informant's uncle and the old man. I ran an NCIC III on both of them, including a Washington driver's check. Both had extensive criminal histories ranging from petty thefts to aggravated assault. I contacted the Tacoma Police Department and the Pierce County Sheriff's Office, asking for them to check their records for all past contacts with the suspects. From the information they provided, I was able to obtain the last known address for the old man Jimmy Smith, and some of his relatives.

It had been almost three months and it had consumed most of my time. I had let most of my other cases go un-worked and I was still getting new ones every day. I told my Sergeant that I was going to spend the day in the Tacoma area, trying to track down the informant's uncle and the old man. He said he wanted to go along, and this surprised me, since he rarely got involved in any of the investigations. Maybe he just wanted to get out of the office and get a free lunch on the county, I don't know.

We spent the entire day talking to family members of the old man, only to find that he had died three years prior. Most of those whom we spoke with remembered Fred's uncle and all of them had stories about his craziness and violet temper. For the most part, we gained very little information that helped the case. The old man would have been our key witness, and probably the least culpable, therefore, I was hoping to get him to turn State's evidence against the other two. This investigation was turning into an emotional roller coaster. Every time I thought I was getting close, something popped up to set me back.

The following day when I arrived at my office, I had a message from a female who said she wanted to talk to me about the case involving the victim. A number was left and I immediately called, reaching an elderly female who identified herself as Bonnie Jackson. (Not her real name) She had read the story in the paper about the discovery of the remains. She said that she had been the hairdresser of the wife of the suspect until they moved back East. She thought she may have some information that I may be interested in, but wanted to talk to me in person. I made arrangements to meet with her at her coastal home the next day.

This had been the only possible break since I received the call from the informant over three months ago. It was a two hour drive to the coast, and I spent the time thinking about possible questions I would ask Bonnie Jackson. I had no idea what kind of information she had for me and for all I knew, it may not even be worth the drive.

When I arrived at the address I had been given, I was greeted by Bonnie Jackson and invited in. It didn't take long before I knew this lady had a lot more information than I had hoped for. She told me that she met the suspect and his wife right after they moved to the coast in the early part of 1984. She had become close friends with the wife and had become her confidant. She said the wife had confided in her that her husband may have killed a woman in Lewis County and that the police had questioned him about it. She said that the wife had told her that shortly after they moved to the coast, her husband had found a note on his truck from the informant's uncle. He was demanding his money, and she thought it was for his help in the murder. Bonnie told me that the suspect's wife had told her that he had bragged about putting a penny in the bottom of his shoe and that in some way prevented him from failing the polygraph. She said the suspect's wife told her that she was afraid of him and at the time, was seeing an attorney about a divorce. It was at this time that I learned that the suspect's wife had died shortly after going back East. Bonnie had called her one day and the suspect had answered the phone, telling her that his wife had passed away. "Crap! Another witness dead."

It wasn't much, but it fit with what I had so far regarding the suspect and Fred's uncle being prime suspects. At the time that the victim disappeared, her boyfriend was the only one that had a real motive. I knew he had met Fred's uncle at the Johnson's residence and made the comment that he would like to see her dead. The denim coat found with the remains fit the description of the coat he wore fishing. The coat had been identified by the suspect's son, and the victim's family was adamant that she never had or even wore a coat of that type. The suspect conveniently told his son that he had lost the coat and had no idea how it ended up with the remains.

On the way back to Lewis County I decided that I would review the original file again and update the new file so everything was current. I wanted to follow up on a few loose ends that included contacting one of the District Court Judges. He had represented the suspect during a civil dispute with the victim. All information in the file had to be substantiated or eliminated. I wanted to get rid of any distractions, thus bringing the investigation to focus in one direction and only on the primary suspects.

The next day I contacted the Judge and talked to him about the suspect. He said he kept all his old files in boxes in his garage and that he would locate the file. I knew this could take a few days, but it would give me a chance to bring my reports up to date.

On Monday I received a call from the Judge. He had found the file and provided me with a copy. It substantiated the dispute between the suspect and the victim over money. The victim had allowed him to park his mobile home on her property next to her house. She had not charged him rent, but he had paid for putting in a septic tank. After their break up, he began to pressure her to reimburse him for the cost of the installation of the septic tank. She maintained that because she had not charged him rent, she didn't owe him anything. A settlement or judgment was never reached before she disappeared.

There was one more thing I wanted before I went much further; a hair sample from the suspect. I called Emily and asked her if she was still willing to help me. She was quick to confirm her desire to help in any way she could. I asked if she thought she could get a few hair samples from the suspect. She wanted to know how she should go about this. I had to refrain from telling her to "just grab a handful and tear it out of the jerk's head." I even smiled as I pictured her doing just that. Instead, I told her that she might try finding some in his bathroom sink or tub, and maybe even a comb or hair brush. I told her that if she was successful, that she was to place them in a paper bag and take them to the Lieutenant at the Police Department. I assured her that I would let the Lieutenant know and that he would be expecting her.

The loose ends were now tied up as much as possible and it was time to contact the suspects. I knew where he was so I concentrated on locating Fred's uncle. In going through his Washington criminal records, I located a former girlfriend who lived in the Tacoma area. I called her and she was a little reserved about discussing him. She was afraid of him and didn't want him finding out that she had talked to me. She did tell me that she had a restraining order against him because he still occasionally tried to harass her by calling or sending her letters. She told me the last she heard he was on the East coast near a brother. She said that she knew he had been in prison and that he was still on probation. I thought it was quite a coincidence that he and the other suspect were both back East.

The next step was to contact the Department of Corrections and verify his probation. After several calls and numerous transfers, I was finally put in touch with his Probation Officer. Lisa was a great help to me and over the next several weeks, she was doing everything she could to locate him for me. She told me that he had failed to show for his last appointment with her and she suspected that he may be on his way to Tacoma, Washington. Finally she called me with what she thought was reliable information. She said that she had found out through his brother that he had in fact, headed for Tacoma, Washington a few weeks before. She said that the brother had mentioned the suspect wanting to reopen an old Labor and Industries claim in Washington for a back injury.

I contacted Washington Labor and Industries in Olympia and learned that he had recently reopened his old claim. Through these records I learned the name of the doctor who had originally treated him in Tacoma. I called the doctor and explained why I wanted to contact his patient. I told him that his patient was a suspect in a murder investigation and that he also had an outstanding warrant for his arrest. After I told the doctor about the history of violence and the possible risks associated in arresting him, the doctor agreed to call his patient and change his appointment. I told him I would get back with him as soon as I could get everything in order.

I contacted the Sergeant with the Major Crimes Unit of the Tacoma Police Department. I'll refer to him as Sergeant Jones. I told him I had a location on a possible co-suspect in a murder and I wanted him arrested on the Tacoma warrant. I explained that I really wanted to interrogate him in regards to the murder. After I gave Sergeant Jones all the information, he assured me that he would assist me in making the arrest. I told him about my conversation with the doctor, and Sergeant Jones told me he would set everything up and would call me in a couple of days.

True to his word, two days later I got the call from Sergeant Jones. He told me that the doctor had called his patient and changed the appointment, asking him to come in the following day at 12:30 p.m. He said that the doctor's staff would be out to lunch and there would be no patients at the office, since it would normally be lunch time. This was great foresight and planning on the part of the doctor and Sergeant Jones to ensure the safety of the office staff and patients. Sergeant Jones told me to meet him at the Police Department the next morning at 11:00 a.m. for a briefing and an opportunity to meet the team that would be making the arrest.

The next morning when I walked into the Tacoma Police Department briefing room, I was not prepared for what I saw. Remember, I was used to Lewis County and the half-assed methods we used to assist other agencies. What I saw was a group of thirteen sober-faced officers who looked like they were ready for anything. Absent was the joking and everyone talking at the same time that I was used to. Sergeant Jones introduced me to the team and asked me to give them a little background about the murder. After I completed presenting my information, Sergeant Jones walked to a large chalk board. On it was a detailed map depicting the doctor's office, surrounding streets and parking lots. He went through the plan that he had in place. Each officer had a specific task and each officer was asked to repeat what his job was, in detail. An arrest team consisted of six of the bigger officers whose tasks were to take down the suspect when the signal was given. A pursuit vehicle would be staged one block away in case the suspect made a run for it in his vehicle. A K-9 unit would be hiding behind the hedges less than one hundred feet from the entrance to the doctor's office in case the suspect ran. Two plain clothed officers would be waiting just inside the door of the Doctor's Office, watching through the glass door. One officer would be in an unmarked car in the parking lot to pull in behind the suspect's car when he started for the office. This would prevent the suspect from making it back to the car in case he alerted on any one of the officers and made a break for it. I would be in the command car with Sergeant Jones and we would be across the street in a parking lot.

I was totally impressed with the extent and expertise used in planning the arrest. But, being the kind of person who always wants to do his own part, I felt left out. However, they treated me like a guest and I never had to lift a finger.

At about 12:30 p.m. every officer was in position and waiting for the suspect. As I look back on that day I realize the suspect never had a chance. At about 12:50 p.m. the suspect drove into the doctor's office parking lot. Sergeant Jones gave the order for all units to get ready. Just as the suspect walked past the rear of his vehicle, the unmarked car eased in behind his car, eliminating any chance of it leaving. It was like watching a movie, only you knew what the next scene was going to be and this was for real. As I watched the suspect walk toward the office, I visualized the officer in the pursuit vehicle, engine running, and ready to take off in pursuit. I could sense the K-9 officer and his partner, every nerve tense and ready to spring into action. I knew the take down team was probably pumping huge quantities of adrenalin as they waited for the signal that was seconds away.

Just as the suspect approached the single step leading to the office door, Sergeant Jones gave the command to move in. The two officers inside stepped outside in front of him, their weapons drawn and pointed directly at his chest. They were giving orders to get on the ground. The six man arrest team seemed to appear from nowhere.

They drove the suspect to the ground and hand cuffed him before he could comprehend what had just happened. The poor guy never knew what hit him.

The suspect was arrested on the outstanding warrant and taken to the Tacoma Police Department. He was placed into an interview room and advised of his warrant. At no time did anyone mention anything about the murder to him. This was something I wanted to spring on him unexpectedly. I was hoping the sudden unexpected resurrection of the old murder would place him at such a disadvantage that he would stumble and confess.

I walked into the room and introduced myself. I read him the required Miranda warnings even though I knew the Tacoma officers had already done that. He started talking about the warrant and I cut him off in mid sentence. I remained calm and spoke in a slow soft voice, hoping to make him a little more comfortable. Then I told him I wanted to talk about the lady that he had helped kill in 1983. For just the briefest of time I saw panic in his eyes. I knew that I had hit something very close to home with him. He stammered, "I don't know what you are talking about." I had to keep the momentum going so I told him about finding the remains, how I had taped a phone conversation with the victim's boyfriend, about the statements I had from witnesses, and how I knew about the note he left on the truck.

Nothing I said made him move from his denials. He agreed to take a polygraph, and I told him I would have it for him within minutes. He had no way of knowing that I already had a paleographer waiting down the hall. He took the test and it ended up being inconclusive. That was as good as a fail as far as I was concerned. Damn it! So close, and yet one more step backwards.

I went back to Chehalis and within a few days the suspect was extradited back to the East coast. I was learning just how hard it is to break through someone's resolve when they have had thirteen years to become entrenched in their alibis. Considering the stakes at risk for both suspects, they may have even come to believe their own story to some degree after that much time.

The next few weeks went by with nothing new developing in the investigation. It was time to pay the victim's former boyfriend a visit. Based on everything I had learned, I was confident that both suspects had killed her. The boyfriend had the motive, the means and the opportunity.

To compound the problem, key witnesses were dead and the lab had provided their report which stated there was no trace evidence, not even a fish scale from the coat.

The next day I made flight reservations for a three day trip to the East coast. I hoped for the best possible outcome, and that was to talk a suspect into confessing. Even with the best-laid plans, there is always the unexpected to contend with and you never know what it will be, or where it will come from. I could prepare an interviewing strategy and study it in detail, but the results were never predictable. At best I could increase the odds a little in my favor by being prepared as much as I could.

September 12, the Boeing 747 left Seattle en route to Chicago. I had my notes so I spent the entire flight studying them, trying to anticipate what the victim's former boyfriend's responses and answers may be. For every one that I came up with, I formulated a counter move. I had tried to profile him based on the information I had and from the information given me by his family. I knew that he was an accomplished liar who never changed his stories or admitted to a lie. I knew that he had a temper, a violent personality, and never felt remorseful after assaulting a family member. I also knew that if he and his accomplice kept to their denials, we would never arrest either of them. Either way, I knew the investigation was coming to a close and a thirteen year old murder would soon be put to rest, with or without an arrest.

When I arrived in Chicago, I had to get to the other end of the airport in order to catch my remaining flight to the city were the suspect resided. The airport is huge and there were thousands of people working their way through the terminals. I had to run at times when there was an opening in the crowds, and was exhausted when I got to the boarding area for my flight. They had just finished boarding and were getting ready to close the door. I was lucky I even made it.

When I got to my destination, I picked up my rental car and drove straight to the Hotel I had reserved. It was 6:15 p.m. and I was tired so I checked into my room, showered and went to bed. When I got up the next morning I went through some minor planning, setting my schedule for the day. The first thing after breakfast I went to the Police Department and met the Lieutenant. He gave me directions to the suspect's residence and even had a patrol unit drive by to make sure the suspect was home.

He told me he would have a unit parked nearby watching the residence, in case I needed anything.

My brain was working at Mach II as I drove to the suspect's residence. I was running the questions through my mind and trying to force myself to be calm at the same time. As I pulled into the driveway I reached under my jacket and unsnapped my holster, making sure my Glock 9 mm would come out quickly, if needed. I never believed you could be too careful and I was completely prepared to shoot him if he attempted any kind of assault. When I stepped out of the car I noticed a brown sedan about half way down the block. I could see someone in the driver's seat, and knew this must be the unmarked unit the Lieutenant had told me about. I walked up to the front door and knocked, noticing that all the blinds were closed. I had no reason to suspect that he knew I was coming but I had an eerie feeling that I was being watched. All these months of hard work and sleepless nights were now cumulating to the point of no return! Within a few seconds the door opened and I was standing face to face with the man whom I believed was the killer from 13 years before. I paused for a moment as I stared into his eyes before I asked if he was, (name left out), and he said he was. I identified myself, showing him my Sheriff's identification. I asked if I could come in and talk with him and he said, "Yes, come on in and follow me out to the patio." He didn't seem at all surprised or inquisitive about why a Detective from Lewis County, Washington had showed up on the East coast to talk to him. I wondered if his accomplice had gotten in touch with him. We went out onto a covered patio just off the back of the house. He sat down in a recliner and I sat down in a chair directly in front of him. I tried to move the chair as close as I could, wanting him to feel pressured. I asked him if he knew why I was there and he answered with a simple "no." I could tell that he was guarded and was going to be a difficult interview. "When was the last time you saw your old friend?" (The accomplice) I asked, watching his eyes closely for a reaction. There was not even a second's hesitation before he answered "Who's that?" I said, "You remember him." He's the one who helped you kill Donna Jean" I replied. You can't hit a suspect any harder or more direct than that, and I wanted to rattle his cage to get him responding with some kind of emotions. His reply was matter of fact, "I didn't kill her," and there was no emotion what so ever. It went on like that for the next three hours. No matter what I said, I couldn't get him ticked off. Normally an innocent person would have told me to go screw myself or ordered me to get the hell off their property. He never did either, and he never admitted to anything. As I looked into his eyes I thought, "This is the coldest human being I've ever met." The nearest I got to getting a rise out of him was when I told him that I would eventually be back for him with an arrest warrant for the murder of Donna Jean. His eyes narrowed slightly and the veins started to stick out on his neck. He just stared at me, never blinking or saying anything. I got up and went to my car, the hairs on the back of my neck standing straight up as I turned my back to him. In my mind, I could almost hear and feel a bullet ripping into my back. It was a short distance from the front door of the house to my car, but it felt like a very, very long walk.

When I got back into my car, I noticed the unmarked unit start up and drive towards me. As it slowly went by the driver waved and I gave him the thumbs up sign, indicating everything was ok. I went back to my hotel room feeling exhausted from the three hours of tension. It always amazed me how physically exhausting these types of interviews could be. It was about 2:00 p.m. and I decided to call Lisa, the Probation Officer. I was surprised when she told me that her subject was in the hospital in Eau Clair, Wisconsin. He was recovering from a back operation, apparently the one he had intended to get in Tacoma before he was "pig piled" into the concrete. After hanging up the phone I called the hospital in Eau Clair and confirmed that he was still there. I advised the hospital administration that I would be there the following day to see him. I gave them only the necessary information that was needed to ensure that I would get to see him when I arrived without any interference.

The next morning I was on the road before 7:00 a.m. It was a full day's drive to the hospital so I had a lot of time to think. I wondered if homicide Detectives ever came to terms with not solving a murder investigation. This one bothered me because I truly believed that I had solved it, but it didn't look like there would ever be an arrest. I think that knowing who committed a murder and not being able to make an arrest is the hardest to accept.

I arrived at the hospital later that day. I didn't waste any time and went straight to his room after a brief check in at the nurse's station. The look on his face was priceless when I walked in and said, "Remember me?" I told you I would be seeing you again." I thought I saw him start to tremble a little and I knew he was rattled. I told him I had just left his friend's and that his friend had told me everything. He just stared at me, his eyes filling with tears. "Finally, one of them is going to break" I thought. I told him that his friend gave him up and was saying that he had killed the woman 13 years ago. I tried to convince him that unless he told me what really happened, that he would go down alone for the murder. I told him that I knew that his friend had helped, and may have been the one who actually killed her. I suggested that perhaps he had been the victim of his friend's manipulation and that perhaps he had only helped dispose of the body. The only thing that he would say is, "I don't know anything." Was it possible that he and the other suspect had done enough research to know how police interviews went? Did they know that we could and would play one against each other? If they had done their research and homework, then they were applying what they had learned very well and holding fast to it. After about an hour it was apparent that he was not going to give it up. There was nothing to do but head back to Washington.

It was a long trip home and I was no closer to making an arrest than I was the day I got the call from this suspect's nephew. I knew it was going to be hard for Donna Jean's family to accept that the murderers were going to remain free. I could only hope that they got some closure in knowing what had happened. At least now they could bury her remains and no longer have to agonize over her whereabouts.

So now we had two murderers from the Mossyrock shooting, plus two from the recovered remains of the missing female, walking free. Four murderers walking free, who had committed their crimes in Lewis County, Washington, and who had been investigated by the same Detective Division.

From Performance Evaluation.....

........Very enjoyable to work with. He has the maturity and spark combination that just naturally makes him an extra special officer. The three letters attached, recognitions of jobs well done, from Pam Jorstad, CCD (Chief Criminal Deputy) Gordan[sic] Spanski, and myself show kindness, a willingness to do a good job, and a willingness to carry through a project given to him. The monthly statistics show a well above average worker. I would have no prob-

lem recommending Jerry for a position as a Corporal or an FTO (Field Training Officer)

Sergeant D. Withrow

10

BETTY SMITH MURDER
1996

BETTY SMITH WAS an elderly lady who lived in a nice mobile home park near Napavine, WA. The Fire Department was called in the middle of the night to her home, which was nearly fully engulfed in flames. When the firefighters made entry, they found the elderly female on the floor. She was brought out to the ambulance and it was then that they discovered she had been shot. She was pronounced dead at the scene. One of the new Detectives was assigned to be the lead investigator. I was not involved in the investigation but from time to time, mostly at the weekly Detective meetings, we would all be briefed as to his progress. There never was any real progress and he always seemed to be going in a different direction with the investigation. He waited two weeks after the murder before setting up a road block to field interview anyone driving that particular road near the residence where Betty lived. This is something that should have been started the same night the incident occurred.

To make a long story short, two years went by and nothing had been accomplished. During that two year period I had become familiar enough with the case to believe that it could be solved. I went to the Sheriff and requested permission to organize a special task force to work on the case. The Sheriff granted me the request. I selected three in the Department who I had worked with and believed to be the best the Department had to offer. I made the selection of the three deputies to assist me and the other Detectives. We pulled the original case file and started our review.

Within two weeks the case was cleared with an arrest of both juvenile suspects. One is still in prison at the time this book was published. The remaining suspect was not charged, much to our dismay. The little punk is still walking free!

I, along with those who worked this case, never understood why the original Detective never solved the murder with an arrest; given the fact that he had the same information we had two years later. The Sheriff had the audacity to call this Detective up, along with my team, for recognition during a presentation in front of the Department. And worse yet, the Detective walked to the front of the room with us and took part in taking credit for something my team accomplished. He took credit for a murder solved that he had not been capable of solving. Instead of the Sheriff asking the Detective why he had not solved the case in the first place, he allowed him to take undue credit.

11

AMANDA REISS MURDER
NAPAVINE, WA
1996-1997

JANUARY 15, 1996, and it looked like it was going to be a nice day outside. It had stopped raining and this time of the year in the Northwest you appreciate a break in the rainy season. I made it the full distance of 30 miles from my residence to the Sheriff's Office without making a traffic stop. I was one of the few Detectives who made regular traffic stops, even though I drove an unmarked car and wore a suit. I've had people pass me at high rates of speed, pass on the wrong side, "tailgating", and a host of other violations; because they didn't know I was law enforcement. Guess they never associated the exempt license plates and multiple antennas with a possible unmarked police car.

After I arrived at my office, the day started pretty much like any other. I reviewed the new cases the Detective Sergeant assigned to me, prioritized them and began the task of finishing up a report on a theft case I had just cleared. It was around 11:00 am when the Sergeant came into the office and told us that human remains had been found in a brushy area near Exit 63 just off Interstate 5. He told us that some brush cutters had come upon the remains and called 911. The Chief Criminal, along with the Undersheriff, had responded to the scene and verified that the remains were human. My Sergeant said he would be going back to the scene with them to "take a look." I asked him if he wanted me to get the crime scene van ready and respond. He said no, that there was no hurry and that "we will start tomorrow." I thought, "Yeah, that makes sense, let's wait and maybe it will be raining again tomorrow." After all, who wants to work in dry weather? I suggested that we should at least secure the scene. My Sergeant said that the remains had been there for several months and that "they aren't going anywhere." At this time, I had not been involved with investigating a death where the remains were badly decomposed and unrecognizable. According to what the Sergeant was telling us, there wasn't much left of the body.

The next morning when I arrived at the office, the Sergeant called the Detectives into the conference room. As we sat down at a long table, he gave us his plans for the day. He told us that we were all to meet at the Park and Ride at Interstate 5 and the Winlock-Toledo road at Noon. He said that he had invited some of the other local agencies to go along. He explained that since the police officers of the local cities had never had a chance to see "crime scenes like this" he thought it would be nice to invite them along. He told us that the Washington State Patrol Total Station team would be there, the lab tech from the State Crime Lab, Centralia Police Department Detectives, Chehalis Police Department Detectives, the on-duty State Patrol Troopers, and the Evidence Custodian. The briefing ended and we were told to be there at Noon. At this point, no one knew who the lead Detective was going to be.

I and two of the other Detectives decided to take one car and Jim agreed to drive. When we arrived at the Park and Ride, it looked like some kind of convention. There were vehicles lined up, trunks open, doors open, and people everywhere. Some were drinking coffee and smoking cigarettes, while other were just milling around. We stopped and just sat there looking at the activity that was going on. The Sergeant wasn't kidding when he said he had invited some others to go along. I was sitting in the front passenger seat and Carl was sitting in the back when the Sergeant arrived in his station wagon. He pulled up along side so his driver's door was directly across from our driver's door. With the driver's window down, it made for easy communicating between the occupants of the two vehicles. Our Sergeant looked like a kid with a new toy, smiling and joking. I am sure his pleasure was related to being out of the office in nice weather with co-workers more than it was anything else. I personally thought the whole thing was looking more like a fiasco. He asked if everyone was there and I wondered who else he was expecting, the President? Jim asked him, who was going to be the lead Detective on this one. The Sergeant looked a little surprised and I believe he must have realized that he had forgotten something. He hesitated a few seconds, then like a light bulb coming on with a new idea, he said "Jerry can be the lead on this one, it's his turn." Jim didn't seem to care one way or the other, but it was my opinion that Carl didn't like it. And to tell the truth, I sure as hell didn't like it either. I didn't want any part of this investigation just from the way it had begun. It wasn't starting out like a serious death investigation by any stretch of the imagination. It was more like a damn circus!

When the Sergeant got everyone lined up, we started the short drive to the body site on the small dirt road which was more like a path than anything. The area had been logged many years before and was now thick with head high brush and thickets. There were places where garbage had been dumped, old appliances, car parts and household waste. I was getting more upset by the minute as I watched the caravan work its way down the path. Our Sergeant lead the way in his station wagon, followed by the Washington State Patrol Total Station team, the crime lab technician, the Centralia Detectives, Chehalis Detectives, the Evidence Custodian with the crime scene van, and the Sheriff's Detectives. I counted seven vehicles and thirteen people going into a crime scene with not even a pretext of interest in crime scene preservation. When the vehicles stopped and everyone started getting out of their vehicles, I wanted to just turn and walk away. To me this was the most embarrassing thing I had seen from the Sheriff's Office. I wasn't a seasoned investigator at the time, but I knew when a body is discovered it became a crime scene, no matter how long it had been there. And any crime scene should be treated as such. That means it should be secured immediately and entered only by the lead investigator and those he appoints for specific duties, and above all taken seriously. I avoided getting involved and stayed around the evidence van as much as possible. I assisted the clerk in bagging the evidence that was brought to us, which consisted of various pieces of debris and some small pieces of bone that had been found.

Finally the day ended and I was glad to get the hell out of there. The two Detectives with me had made several comments that indicated to me that they would have preferred being the lead on this one. They had no idea at the time just how much I would have preferred that either one of them was. And if I had my way, one of them was going to be the lead. The next morning when I arrived at the office, I went straight to my Sergeant. I told him that I didn't want to be the lead on this investigation, and that "I sure as hell didn't need the other Detectives patronizing me." I told him that Carl seemed to think he was the better investigator and I would just as soon he took the lead. I also told him how ridiculous I thought it had been to wait until we all arrived at the scene to make the lead assignment. I told him that I didn't like the way it had been "dumped" on me without having had the opportunity to be involved in the way the initial response was conducted. He seemed a little embarrassed at the mention of the response we had made the day before. He surprised me by saying, "I guess I could have done things differently" and then said, "You are going to stay as the lead Detective and the others will assist you as you need it." He then had the others come into the office and he made it clear that I was going to remain the lead Detective. He made a point of telling the others that they would assist me in whatever capacity I needed. It wasn't hard to tell from the look on their faces that this was not to their liking.

I spent the rest of the day making notes and trying to formulate a plan for the investigation. We had some very badly decomposed remains of a human being and the gender, age, and race was unknown. We didn't know if it was a local person or an out-of-the-area victim that had just been dumped in Lewis County. It wouldn't be the first time that a body had been dumped in Lewis County when the murder had occurred in another part of the state.

The following morning I went to the Coroner's office and looked at the remains. There was not much to work with. There were a few small bones that appeared to be vertebrae, a femur, portion of an upper thigh and quadriceps, the radials, jaw, and some tissue. The teeth would be the saving grace in identification. I still didn't know what we were going to do with the remains at this point. I knew that the bones would have to be stripped of all flesh and cleaned in order to attempt to lay them out in an effort to reconstruct the skeleton. I just didn't know exactly how that was going to be done.

I went back to my office and ordered a copy of the Missing Persons reports for the past year. I then sent out a nationwide teletype describing what we had and asking for any agency with a missing person to respond. I called the Forensic Orthodontist and made arrangements to bring the jaw with the teeth to his office for identification. Until the remains were identified, there was no clear direction to go. For all we knew, the cause of death could be anything from natural causes to murder, and either one could have occurred anywhere in the nation. It had obviously been several months since the person had died.

I talked to my Sergeant about cleaning the skeletal remains and he suggested boiling them to remove the flesh. He told me to get with the Evidence Custodian and she could help. So, I contacted the Evidence Custodian, and told her what he had suggested. She didn't have a clue as to how or where we were going to perform this "boiling" technique. She suggested that she could possibly buy a very large pot and that we could do it someplace where no unsuspecting citizen could happen upon the process. I have to tell you that I had a vision of us standing around a large black witches pot hanging from a tri-pod boiling bones! The more it was discussed, the more absurd it sounded. The others thought it was funny and made several jokes about it, however, it just seemed a little too primitive to me. The Lewis County Coroner's Office did not have at the time, and still does not have, a Medical Examiner. With that said, the Coroner's office had nothing to offer in the way of advice or help. I have often referred to the Lewis County Coroner's office as nothing more than a "body pick-up service." In fact, in my 13 years of law enforcement in Lewis County, and the many death scenes I had responded to, I never once saw the elected Coroner at one. Never! He always sent his deputies, and most often it was the beauty shop operator who was his chief deputy. I always joked that at least, "the corpses could have a pretty hair-do."

I called several Pathologists and finally connected with one in the Portland, Oregon area. I told him what we had and asked if he could help us. He told me to bring the remains to him and that he would clean them and lay them out in correct order so they could be photographed. This was a huge relief, knowing that we would get the necessary work done by a professional.

The Pathologist agreed to meet with us on Saturday, so I made the necessary arrangements with the Coroner's office. The arrangements consisted of letting the Deputy Coroner know that she would have to be at the Coroner's office Saturday so I could pick up the remains. It was left up to me to get the remains to Portland any way I could. My first plan was to put the camper shell on my pick-up truck in order to at least conceal the body bag from the public eye. I could just imagine getting stopped by some Trooper on the freeway and explaining why I had human remains in the back of my truck. I knew that the Sheriff's Office had the evidence van, which is nothing more than a converted ambulance. At least it was marked as a Law Enforcement vehicle and would raise less suspicion than my personal truck hauling a body bag. I contacted the Evidence Custodian, and told her I would be using the evidence van on Saturday. On more than one occasion I have watched Deputy Coroners in Lewis County shove bodies into the back of their personal vehicles. You would think that a professional Sheriff's Office and Coroner's Office in this day and age would have a better method of transporting human remains.

My son, Rowdy had just become a Reserve Deputy with the Sheriff's Office, so I contacted him and asked if he would like to go on with me Saturday. He jumped at the chance to assist in the investigation in any manner he could. He was 27 years old and trying hard to get his foot in the door of law enforcement. I thought it would be a great training session for him, plus it would be an opportunity for him to get a close look at what homicide investigations were really like.

I then contacted one of the Reserve Deputies, Ben, who was a part time professional Geologist. I asked him about performing a forensic type dig at the site where the remains had been found. I knew professional agencies used the method and we were going to need everything we could get if we ever hoped to solve this case. He immediately agreed and was enthusiastic about helping in the investigation. I told him I would make the necessary arrangements and get back to him with the date and time.

When Saturday arrived, Rowdy met me at my residence and we headed for the Sheriff's Office. We picked up the evidence van and then drove over to the Coroner's office. The beautician was waiting for us and she opened the large roll-up garage door so I could back the van in. The remains were still in the body bag that they had originally been placed in, so all we had to do was pull it from the cooler and load it into the back of the van. In a few minutes we were on Interstate 5, heading South to Portland. It was a two hour drive so I spent the time telling Rowdy everything I knew about the case, so far. When I told him that I had talked to Ben about excavating the body site, he was quick to ask if he could go along and help. I told him he could, and told him that we would be searching for evidence while the Reserve was excavating. He could help me with that, as well as bagging and logging in anything we found. Having him help me was a lot better than the help (or lack thereof) that I was getting from anyone else.

When we arrived at the lab in Portland, we were greeted by the Pathologist. The remains were unloaded and placed onto the typical stainless steel table. As the Pathologist started sorting the remains from the various pieces of debris, I looked around the large room, noticing that there were several other examining tables. It was always a refreshing experience to get away from Lewis County and see modern facilities and true professionals. We watched as the Pathologist carefully scrubbed and washed each bone until it was thoroughly clean and placed onto the table. Each bone was placed in what would have been its correct anatomical position. There was no "boiling," "no fire", just careful cleaning with a soft bristle brush and cleaning solution.

About an hour into the process, two more Pathologists arrived and, shortly after that, two bodies were brought in and placed on tables. The body on the table next to ours was that of a large woman who had been found dead along side one of the railroad tracks in the Portland area. The other body was that of an African American male who had been dead for several days before being found. The body was bloated and starting to change colors in places. It was not a pleasant site and the odor was rank! I watched Rowdy's face to see his reactions. He had a somber expression; a little pale, but other than that he was doing ok. Three autopsies at one time and the Pathologist chatting like any one else would on a Saturday at work. I kept glancing over at Rowdy when the electric saw started removing the top of the skull from the male body. A small amount of bone fragments were flying off the blade and Rowdy stepped back a few paces, which put him closer to the table with the female body. The chest cavity of the female had been opened and it was at about this time that the Pathologist's Assistant accidentally ruptured a breast implant. The liquid silicone shot toward Rowdy like being shot from a squirt gun. The pathologist said, "Oops," Rowdy said, "Shit" and I started laughing! Poor Rowdy, all he knew was there were small bone fragments spraying from the saw that was removing the top of a head, an open chest with internal organs in a pan resting on the legs of a corpse, and liquid being shot at him from the body. I was proud of him! He was white as a sheet and doing his best not to throw up while backing toward the door, all the while pretending to be going outside for a cigarette. I knew then that he was going to make it as a cop. This was way more than the average person would, or should have to be exposed to this early in their career.

At the end of the day, the Pathologist was able to determine that the remains were most likely that of a female, probably early teens. He estimated her height to be approximately five feet. There were no telling signs of injury to any of the bones that would indicate the cause and manner of death. There were gnawing marks that were contributed to being caused by small animals, but that was all. We put the skeletal remains in a clean bag and went back to Lewis County.

Monday morning I received a call from the Orthodontist. He had identified the dental remains as belonging to Amanda Reiss. Identification was positive and he would be sending an official report to me within a few days. This matched with one of the missing reports I had pulled days earlier from the Records Department.

I started creating the flow charts once the skeletal remains had been identified as those of thirteen year old Amanda Reiss. She had been reported missing in August 1996, but because she had a history of running away, the Sheriff's Office would not investigate her disappearance. According to Amanda's mother and grandmother, the Sheriff's Office told them Amanda was not missing, that she was a runaway. I never found anything in any of the reports I read that indicated the Sheriff's Office did or did not do this. The Coroner's office made the notification to the family, the one thing they seemed capable of doing.

The following day, I contacted Amanda's grandmother, who Amanda had been staying with at the time of her disappearance. She told me that on the night of August 6, 1996, she had left Amanda home when she went to play cards at a nearby friend's house. While there, Amanda had called her and told her that "Harry was there" and he was going to help her cut some frozen bacon so she could cook her dinner. Harold Hawkins was a longtime family friend and she didn't think anything about him being there. She had Amanda put Harold on the phone and spoke to him for a few minutes. Since Harold spent much of his time at the Reiss house, she was not concerned. She said Amanda sounded like "herself" and there was no indication that anything was wrong. Later that night when she arrived back home, Amanda was gone. Her first thought was that her daughter had come and picked up Amanda. She called her daughter and found out that Amanda was not with her. She then thought that Amanda must have run away and she would call soon, as she had in the past. The following day, she called the Sheriff's Office and apparently was told that there was nothing that could be done because they believed Amanda to be a runaway.

I interviewed Amanda's uncle while I was there, who had grown up with "Harry" and was told the following: Harold was a frequent visitor at the Reiss residence, almost on a daily basis. When he visited, he would sometimes stay several hours, so it was not unusual for him to drop by unexpectedly. I was then told that after Amanda disappeared, "Harry" quit coming by as often, and didn't stay long when he did. He had noticed "Harry" driving by on several occasions without stopping at all, and he thought that was odd.

I went back to the office and updated my report. I was starting to get a little excited, now having a direction to go. I instructed Carl, one of the assisting Detectives, to start locating some of Amanda's friends and begin interviewing them. I added the new information to my flow chart for witness information. I sat at my desk for several hours, reviewing what we now knew.

The victim had been identified as Amanda Reiss. The last known location of the victim had been determined, her grandmother's house. The last known person to see the victim had been determined to be "Harry", who we identified as Harold Dean Hawkins. We knew the location of the body site, so now we needed to spend a few days eliminating any other possible suspects.

Carl had located the name of Amanda's boyfriend who had moved to Texas shortly after Amanda's disappearance. This was a red flag that couldn't be ignored! I had added about 40 names of people I wanted interviewed to the chart. These were names of Amanda's schoolmates and friends that had been accumulated by Carl and me. I told Carl that we would work our way through the list until completed and see what it turned up. Over the next 36 hours, I interviewed 31 of the potential witnesses. My assisting Detective, Carl interviewed five! I have the names of every person I interviewed, as well as the names of the few that Carl interviewed, just as they can be found in the case file. Should anyone request a copy of the file under the Freedom of Information Act, the names would be blackened out, but the numbers would still be the same as they were at the time of the investigation.

Carl was one of those who collected crime scene photos and kept them in albums, much like most people keep family photos. He said he liked to use them for teaching aides. I guess that made sense, but it just seemed a little too weird for me. I had no way of knowing at the time that he would eventually use the Amanda Reiss case as an example of his prowess in a class at the Centralia Community College. Little did he know at the time that my nephew was in that class when he took credit for solving the murder. Yeah, this is the same Detective that couldn't solve the Betty Smith case in two years! But I had the opportunity to be a guest instructor a few weeks later for the same class. I made it a point to provide the class with the truth and the evidence to back it up.

I called Ben, the Reserve, and made arrangements for him to meet me at the body recovery site on Saturday. I then contacted Rowdy and told him we would be looking for more evidence, as well as assisting Ben in whatever way we could Saturday.

Saturday arrived and it looked like rain! Rowdy and I readied the evidence van, making sure the awning covering was in its usual storage place. We would need it to set up over the body site to keep out the rain that was sure to come. I stopped for two cups of coffee to go and Rowdy made sure the camera was loaded with fresh film.

Ben and his assistant were at the Park and Ride at Exit 63 when we arrived. He followed us back into the brush as we drove to the location where the body had been found. We set up the covering over the site and helped with setting up the grid lines that would be used for reference lines to measure the exact location of any evidence that was found.

Rowdy and I spent the rest of the day searching the area for anything that may have been dragged off by animals. We found small bone fragments in several different places on the dirt road that had been missed, during the search the day the Sergeant led the caravan into the scene. It is my opinion that this, in itself, was a testimony to the unfortunate consequences of the inept investigative practices that was so common in the Lewis County Sheriff's Office. By the end of the day, we had several small evidence bags containing various pieces of bones. Ben had found a small hair during his dig; a human hair. This was a remarkable find and was proof of Ben's expertise and diligence in his work. The hair could belong to Amanda or her killer, and could be the one piece of DNA evidence that could make or break the case.

It was about the middle of the week when the Evidence Custodian came to me and told me the following story. She had been to a class on crime scene investigations and evidence collecting. The class had been taught by a Washington State Patrol Crime lab expert. It was the same lab expert who the Sergeant had invited to tag along the first day we went to the site where Amanda had been found. During the class, he had used the Amanda case as an example of, "everything not to do" when arriving at a crime scene. Apparently, he did say toward the end of the class that when he had heard that the Detective in charge had brought in an expert to excavate the site that he knew some things were starting to be done correctly. The clerk said she had been very embarrassed during the class because most of the attendees knew she was from Lewis County.

A few years later when I started bringing all the problems to the surface, I told the Sergeant about this and he became very upset and confronted the Evidence Custodian to see if it was in fact true. When she confirmed it, he even called the lab tech, but would never say what the tech had told him. I have my own suspicions about what the tech told him, and I bet it was not what the Sergeant wanted to hear.

It was time to talk to Harold Hawkins, and I discussed it with Carl. Even though I didn't care for Carl, he was still assigned to assist me and I tried to keep him in the loop. We decided that we would have Harold Hawkins come in so we could get a basic statement from him. Nothing accusatory at this point, but we wanted to find out what he had to say about being with Amanda on the night she disappeared. I placed a call to Harold and he agreed to come in and talk to us.

That afternoon when he came in, I was surprised at his size. He was well over six feet tall and at least 225 pounds. He had a thick mustache, dark shoulder length hair, and seemed a little nervous. But most people are nervous when they are called into a Police Department for a statement, so that alone was not much of a sign of guilt. He sat at a table across from us with his hands clasped together. I told him that we had been taking statements from everyone who knew Amanda and that it was "no big deal". We spent some time getting him to relax a little and then told him that we wanted to get a taped statement. He agreed and when the tape recorder was turned on, the usual introduction was given, including the Miranda warnings. Harold told us that he had stopped at the Reiss residence on the evening in question and Amanda had been the only one home. She had asked him to help her cut some bacon and he agreed. While he was there, Amanda's grandmother called to check on Amanda. Amanda had handed him the phone and he had spoken to Amanda's grandmother. Harold told us that after he finished cutting the bacon, he left and Amanda was cooking the bacon at that time. The statement was short and there were no accusatory questions asked at that time. We thanked him for being so cooperative and let him leave. We now had him locked into a statement, seemingly short and not of much value. However, it was of great value! He had admitted to being with Amanda the night she disappeared, had stated that Amanda was cooking the bacon when he left, and the grandmother had already told us that the bacon was still on the counter uncooked. He was now the primary suspect, but we had to link him to the body dump site. At this time, we couldn't prove he had anything to do with her death.

The next day, I worked on the charts until Noon. One chart showed the last seen location, the body dump site, and the location of Harold's residence. I asked the County Engineering Department to make me a large scaled map that would show the three locations and surrounding areas. It is interesting to see a bird's eye view of the various locations associated with a crime, and how they fit together with time and distance factors.

That afternoon, Carl and I drove out to the Hawkins' residence. We left from the Reiss residence and drove first to the site where Amanda had been found (body dump site). I wanted to know the distance from where she had last been seen (last seen site), to the body dump site. We then drove straight to Hawkins' residence and noted the distance. When we pulled into the driveway, there was a light colored Chevrolet Citation in the driveway. We got out and walked over to the car. As soon as I looked through the window at the inside of the car, I knew we had something. The interior of the car had been removed; seats, door panel, and carpet. There was a pail that appeared to contain some water and a one gallon bleach bottle on the floor board. What better way to attempt to clean up blood than bleach? Carl checked the residence to see if anyone was home while I obtained a telephonic warrant to seize the car. As soon as the Judge approved the warrant and authorized me to affix his signature, I called for a tow truck.

When the tow truck arrived, we made sure that the driver knew what he was dealing with and made sure he did not touch the interior of the car. We had the car towed to the County Maintenance Garage, where we set up yellow tape, barricading the car off. The Washington State Patrol lab tech was requested to respond and process the car.

After the car was secured, at least as secure as it could be in a mechanic's garage for all to see, we went to our offices. I contacted the Search and Rescue Unit and made arrangements for them to meet me on Saturday at the Park and Ride at Exit 63. I advised them that it would be an evidence search and the details would be provided to them at a briefing on Saturday morning.

I then called Harold Hawkins and asked if he could come in the following day and talk to me. He agreed. The next morning, Harold Hawkins arrived at the appointed time and we went through the usual pleasantries for a few minutes. I emphasized how much I appreciated his willingness to help us and it worked well with him. I explained that I needed to ask a few more questions and that it would be the same process as before. I let him know that he was free to go at anytime. He agreed to another taped interview and I read him the Miranda warnings as I did the first time he gave a statement. I told him that we had found his car with the interior stripped and that we had seized it. He said he figured that was the case when he came home and found it gone. I asked him why it was being stripped and he told me the following story: He said that he had been stripping the car and selling the parts. When asked where he had sold them, he said he had sold them to a wrecking yard in Longview. He provided a name for the wrecking yard. When asked about the water and bleach, he said he had wanted to make sure the car was clean before selling the car body. I told him that it all made sense to me and ended the interview. We shook hands and he left, with me thinking how much I hated pretending I was his friend. But, that is the way with the interviewing and interrogation process; making the suspect feel comfortable enough to talk to you. And now we had him locked into another story, his explanation of the car being stripped.

It didn't take long to confirm that there was no such wrecking yard with the name Harold Hawkins had given. We even called the wrecking yards that were listed in the Longview area and confirmed that none of them had purchased any seats or other interior parts for a Chevrolet Citation. No doubt we had our guy in our sites, but we needed some physical evidence to tie him to the body site, and the body to his car.

I went down to the garage and met with the lab tech that was processing the car. He had some good news for us. He had found blood in the car. It was small traces, but had tested positive for human blood using his field-testing equipment. Traces of blood had been found in the threads of the bolts that secured the seatbelts to the floor. The blood, like any liquid had soaked through the carpet and then pooled in the recessed area where the seatbelt bolted through the floor. While still in liquid form, the blood had seeped into the threads of the bolt, working its way through the spiral threads. There were traces of blood found inside the passenger door panel on the bottom of the door frame. These were places that Harold Hawkins had overlooked in his attempt to clean the car. I noticed a very small piece of what appeared to be some kind of glass in the floor. Upon closer examination, it was a crystal like piece, white, and about one quarter the size of an eraser on a pencil. I left the lab tech to his work and headed home; it had been a very long week.

Sunday, I met with the Search and Rescue Units at the Park and Ride as planned. As usual I was alone. I had the large area maps the County Engineering Department had made for me, and they depicted the forest service roads, as well as the County roads. The map showed an area of about 50 square miles with the body dump site as the central location. The members of the search unit gathered around the map display as I explained what I was looking for, and gave them the areas I wanted searched. They were the experts in searching, so I didn't even try to tell them how to perform the searches. I had them start their ground teams at the Park and Ride. They would search the grounds all the way to the site where the body had been found. Training teaches that a killer will often dispose of critical evidence within a few miles of the kill site and dump site. I drew straight lines on the map connecting the three locations. These locations being the Reiss residence, the Hawkins residence, and the body dump site. They formed an uneven triangle, and the average distance of the three lines were about six miles. This indicated to me that Hawkins was not inclined to wander far from home, therefore, I believed that any evidence found would be within the same distance of his home as the average distance of the straight lines I had drawn on the map. With that in mind, I told the search coordinator that I would like the Off Road Vehicle Team to start near the Hawkins residence and work the forest service roads. They were given the description of the bucket seats and other interior parts that Harold Hawkins had removed from his car. For the next hour, I responded to every call from the Ground Team when they came upon any item. They were walking shoulder to shoulder in a long straight line, and every piece of paper, bottle, and foreign object was called out, stopping the entire line until I responded and collected the item found. One thing for sure, they weren't going to miss anything. Many of the searchers were youths who volunteered; some were with the Civil Air Patrol. They deserve a lot of praise and recognition for their dedication and efforts. These kids were awesome!

By the end of the first hour, I received a call on my portable radio from the Off Road team. They had found something and requested I respond to their location. They gave me the location, which was on the first forest service road not far from Hawkins' residence. When I arrived, the team leader told me that they had found a bucket seat fitting the description I had given, and it was about a quarter of a mile up the road inside an old school bus waiting shelter. He said they had found car carpet another quarter mile up the road and a second bucket seat further up the road. I followed them to the old school bus waiting shed. It sat just off the dirt road and was about six foot square in size. The old plank siding was weathered and split and it was obvious that it had not been used in many years. I nearly jumped with excitement when I looked inside. There was a car bucket seat that was the same style and color that would have been in Harold Hawkins' car. I carefully processed the site and collected the seat. There were stains on the seat that appeared to be blood. On the floor, just behind the seat was a small white crystal piece that was similar to the one found in Harold's car. This was very exciting! After finishing, we went up the road a short distance to the location of the carpet. It was also the same color as we were looking for. It had been thrown over a barbed wire fence into a small grassy field on the left side of the dirt road. I collected it and then proceeded up the road about one half mile where the other searchers were waiting. Another bucket seat just like the one already collected, had been thrown over an embankment, landing in a creek about 15 feet below. It was collected and even though it was wet from the creek, it showed stains that appeared to be blood. The seats matched, one left and one right. The carpet matched and the very small white object at the school bus waiting shed appeared to be the same type and size found in Harold Hawkins' car. All the evidence had been found well within the average six mile distance; the pattern Harold Hawkins had established. The day had been a very successful one, thanks to all the great people who participated with the Search and Rescue Unit. I tried to let them all know what an incredible job they had done and the service they had provided to the victim's family.

I made the necessary notifications to the Detective Sergeant, and went home a happy man that night.

The next morning was Monday, and my brain was going 90 miles a minute as I drove to my office. I planned on bringing Harold Hawkins in later in the day for what I figured would be his last interview. I had probable cause for the arrest, and had it since the blood had been found in his car, but I was going for a confession now. When I got to the office I brought my reports up-to-date and briefed Carl on my plans. Now he was suddenly very interested in helping, knowing that an arrest was imminent. I remember thinking to myself, "Where were you over the weekend?" We discussed our options and decided to call Harold Hawkins to see if he would come in again voluntarily.

I called Harold Hawkins and he said he would come in at 6:00 p.m. that afternoon. That gave us time to get our reports caught up and plan our meeting with Harold Hawkins. After I brought my reports up to date, I spent some time getting a room ready for the interview with Harold. I cleaned out a small office that was about eight foot by eight. It had a window the full length of one wall and a door on the opposite wall.

When I finished with the room, it was bare with the exception of three folding chairs. One chair was placed with its back to the window, facing the door. This is where Harold would sit. The other two chairs were placed in front of the single chair with about three feet separating them. Everything was removed from the walls, giving the room a bleak, bare appearance. There was a purpose for all of it, and every bit of training and knowledge we had was going to be needed.

Placing Harold in the chair with its back to the window would put him in a position where he would not be distracted or have anything to focus on. He would be facing the only exit from the room, but between him and the exit, would be the Detectives. The idea in a nut shell was to create an atmosphere that would put pressure on Harold; a feeling of being cornered and trapped. It was coming down to a psychological game with his freedom at stake. I spent the next few hours pouring over the reports, flow charts, and evidence, trying to build on the psychological profile of Harold, based on the previous interviews and witness statements. He was single, pretty much a loner, and didn't have many close friends. He was still living at home with his parents and didn't have a career or work-related skill. He was a man who was quiet and not outspoken, unless he was with those he knew well. He had no known career ambitions and no known plans of any substance for the future. He didn't stray far from his home environment, always staying in the area where he felt comfortable.

Based on these few things the profile that emerged was: A man who was insecure, low self esteem, somewhat immature, not well educated, no long term life plans, and limited life experiences. With this in mind, we decided that the best approach in dealing with him during the final interrogation would be compassion with direct honesty. We had the necessary proof regarding the car being stripped, the blood in his car, and the fact that we knew he had been the last person with Amanda. Trying to bluff, or use any kind of ruse would only lead him to believe that we were still on a fishing expedition. He would have to know we had the facts and could prove them.

The back up plan was that Carl would play the "bad cop" and I would play the "good cop", if necessary. We went through various scenarios and strategies, trying to foresee any potential problems or upsets. I think waiting for this interview was the hardest and longest wait I'd ever had. This was the final leg of the investigation and I knew that whether the killer was going to either walk or stay was dependent on the interview and how well both sides could "play the game."

Finally, Harold came in and I went through the usual pleasantries before leading him into the interview room I had set up just for him. I had everything I needed in a folder lying on the chair I would sit in. I instructed Harold to have a seat and motioned to the chair in front of the window. As soon as he sat down, it was apparent that he was uncomfortable. There was nothing to look at, no table to place his hands on or hide behind. I started with letting him know that I needed to clarify a few things he had told me previously about selling the parts he had stripped from his car. I told him it was no big deal; that I may have misunderstood him the last time he was in. I let him know that it would be the same process as before and that I was going to advise him of his rights. He said, "No problem" as I pulled my Miranda card from my wallet. After advising him of his rights, I asked him to tell me again where he had sold the seats and other car parts. He gave me the same story as before about the wrecking yard near Longview. Without warning, I dropped pictures of the bucket seats at the locations where they had been recovered in his lap. I told him bluntly, "We found all the car parts, there is no such wrecking yard, and Amanda's blood was found in your car." My demeanor was the exact opposite of what he was used to. Suddenly he was confronted with the truth, caught in his lies, and I could see panic in his eyes. After several seconds, and he had not responded, I told him that we knew he had killed Amanda, and the game was over. I told him that the best thing he could do for himself now was to continue to cooperate, and start telling the truth. It was apparent from the look on his face and in his eyes that he was frantically trying to figure out what his next move should be. Harold Hawkins was not the brightest bulb in the lamp, and he would prove to be a textbook example of how well the Reid Interviewing/Interrogation techniques could work. I sat down in the chair directly in front of him; Carl was sitting in the chair to my left. I kept prompting Harold to talk, trying to touch on a theme that might get him to open up. He just sat there, looking beaten and dejected, but he wasn't saying anything. I kept up a constant one way dialogue going. The interviewer cannot allow for any lengthy period of silence when interrogating suspects. Basically, we couldn't give his brain time to "catch up" with all that we were hitting him with. I knew going into the interview this time that it would last until one of two things happened, either he told us the truth, or he invoked his rights. I worked every possible theme I could think of: religion, sports, cars, motorcycles, hobbies, and nothing was getting any spark out of him. Finally, I started blaming Amanda, telling him that I knew how young girls could stir up a man's passions, and that I bet it was all an accident. This got the first response in the two hours since we started. In fact, he was quick to respond with, "That's not what happened." After about 30 minutes, he came forth with the following story: (Story # 2) He said he had stopped at the Reiss residence to visit and found Amanda home alone. She had asked him to come in and help her cut up some frozen bacon. He said he was cutting the frozen bacon when she asked if he would take her for a ride in his car. They left the house and were driving around the rural roads between Napavine and Vader. He went around one corner to fast and the passenger door flew open. Amanda fell out of the car and slid along the gravel shoulder, coming to a stop after hitting a fence post. He said that when he got stopped and went back to check on her, she was dead from hitting her head on the fence post so hard. He said that he put her in the car then panicked, taking her body to where it had been found near Interstate 5. I told him that it made perfect sense to me and that I was sorry he had to go through that. He gave me the location and name of the road where this took place. I told him that I would grab Carl and we would drive over to the location. I told him it would be easy to prove the story because there would be marks and blood on the gravel shoulder, and that there would certainly be evidence on the fence post. He leaned forward and placed his head in his hands, his elbows resting on his knees. Trapped by more lies! It was like a verbal chess game, and I tried to stay one move ahead of him.

I leaned forward and placed my hand on his shoulder, he drew back and it was obvious that he was not going to respond to sympathetic touching. For some, a sympathetic touch will bring forth a flood of emotions.

He then started talking and told us the following: (Story #3) He had stopped by the Reiss residence and Amanda was home alone. She had asked him to come into the house and help her cut some bacon. He went in and while there, Amanda's grandmother called and he spoke with her on the phone for a few minutes. After he got off the phone Amanda had started to play around and fell, stabbing herself with a knife. He put her in the car and started to take her to the hospital when she died. He panicked and took her body out to the area off Interstate 5 and dumped her. He said he was afraid he would be accused of killing her and didn't know what else to do. We were getting near the three hour mark now and I didn't want anyone thinking that Harold was being denied any basic rights. He was taken to the restroom and allowed a break from the small interview room.

Hamburgers were ordered for all of us and while we waited, we kept up the constant dialogue with him. There still could not be that time of silence that might give him time to start thinking too much. After we had eaten, Harold and I went back into the small room. It was time to try the one-on-one method. Carl would remain outside in the hall or in his office nearby.

When we sat down, I reminded Harold of his rights again; moving quickly into a different theme. I touched on the idea of how this was going to hurt his parents. His eyes started to water a little and it was a sign that this was something that was close to him, something that was going to bother him. I told him that his parents would be able to accept that he made a mistake, but that they would not be able to accept him lying about it. I reminded him that he was a good guy that had been raised properly and that his parents would still love him, but needed to at least know the truth. He was getting close to talking, but was having a hard time saying it out loud. The hardest part for most perpetrators is verbalizing their crime. At this point, per a pre-arranged plan, Carl opened the door and asked me to step out. When I stepped out of the room, I left the door ajar just enough to allow Harold to hear everything that was said. Carl started talking in a louder than usual voice, and was doing a good job pretending that he was my supervisor. He told me that we had wasted enough time "with this guy" and that we had "more than enough" to get a conviction. He went on for awhile about how he was ordering me to get the interview "rapped up, and book Harold" so we could go home. I responded in what I tried to make sound like a soft pleading voice, asking that I be allowed to give Harold a chance, that I thought he was basically a good guy. Carl said to "get it done and get him booked." I went back into the room and Harold made no mention of the conversation he had just heard. I told Harold that he could spend most, if not the rest of his life behind bars based on the evidence we had. It took another hour of soft persuasion to get him to give his final version of what occurred that fateful night at the Reiss residence. This is what he told me. (Story # 4) He had stopped at the Reiss residence to visit. Amanda had invited him in and told him that she was the only one home. Amanda asked him to help her cut some bacon that was frozen, and he agreed to help her. None of the knives she had been using were sharp enough, so he used the hunting knife that he had with him. As he was about to start cutting the bacon, Amanda's grandmother called to check on Amanda. Amanda had put Harold on the phone and he spoke with her for a few minutes. After hanging up the phone, he started cutting the bacon. He said Amanda kept teasing him and playing around. She got his wallet from his pants pocket and started teasing him; not giving it back. He turned around quickly and was holding the hunting knife about waist high, extended out in front of him. At the same time Amanda was coming toward him, she tripped and fell forward into the knife. She fell to the floor with the knife stuck in her throat. He said he grabbed her and dragged her out to his car intending to take her to the hospital. He said that when he got her to the car and was trying to get the passenger door open, she kept trying to reach for the knife. He said he was on his knees, pinning her arms to her sides with his right arm. She managed to get one arm free and was trying to get to the knife so he then had to place one knee on her arm to prevent her from pulling the knife out. Once he had her in the car, he started driving, still trying to prevent her from pulling the knife out with his right hand. He said she was trying to speak, making "gurgling sounds" and was pleading with him to help her. He said he panicked, and just kept driving around until she finally quit struggling, and he knew she was dead. He then took her body to the place off Interstate 5 and dumped her. He then went back to the Reiss house and cleaned up the blood and then went home. He said he had went back to the body site about two weeks later to see if it was still there, and it was.

After he finished he just sat staring at the wall. I believed that about 90 % of the story was factual, but there was something he was leaving out. I asked him if he had raped Amanda, then killed her when she threatened to call the police. I approached this angle from different directions, but he stayed with his denial, however there didn't appear to be any real conviction in it. I threw out one last scenario to him and it was basically this: He went to the Reiss residence finding Amanda alone. They engaged in some playful banter, and he became sexually aroused. He raped her, killed her to keep her quiet, and then disposed of her remains. He then made up the story about her "falling on the knife." He wouldn't buy into it, yet he never became angry about being accused of it.

After eight hours of interviewing story number four was his final version. We escorted Harold down to the jail and he was booked for Murder 1st Degree. Three weeks after the body had been discovered, the case was investigated and concluded with the arrest of the killer.

Letter from Detective Chris Fitzgerald.

Centralia Police Department

May 28, 1997
Dear Jerry,
I just wanted to write and let you know what a great job I thougth you did on the Amanda Reiss case. I remember walking into your office about a week into the investigation and seeing the toll the long hours of work were taking on you. The fatigue was written all over your face. The sad part of it was, you were probably the only person losing sleep over the murder of this little girl and despite what anyone else's opinion may be, she was just that, a little girl..........................
I know you must be disgusted at the total apathy that surrounded the violent death of this child. I don't think I can say anything to make you feel better about that. I can tell you though that there is one person who is probably resting better knowing that at least someone cared. That would be Amanda. I think all this little girl ever wanted was someone to care. I also thank you for your hard work. Sometime I'd like to talk to you about how you solved this case. I'm sure I could learn a great deal from you.

Take care Jerry, I hope you are taking pride in a job well done.

Chris Fitzgerald

    The prosecutor, accepted an *Alford* plea from Harold Hawkins and a child killer was given a mere ten years in prison, eligible for parole in just over eight years. The family was horrified and most of us in law enforcement were appalled at such a minimum sentence. An *Alford* plea allows for a suspect to not admit to the crime but agree that the evidence is such, that should it be presented to a jury they would most likely be found guilty. It always struck me as odd that when defense attorneys suspected their clients would be found guilty they pushed for the *Alford* Plea. The prosecutor didn't think the case was strong enough to win a conviction. We had physical evidence, trace evidence, DNA evidence and a confession! And the prosecutor allowed an *Alford* Plea. Perhaps it was just a quick solution to get rid of the necessity of a trial, and still maintain a good conviction rate? Here again I will express my opinion and that is I believe that the prosecutor was more a politician than he was a good public servant.

From Performance Evaluation

........Detective Berry has demonstrated the ability to investigate a variety of cases, from sex crimes and thefts to prosecutor follow-ups and other things I have assigned him. It appears his investigative skills are well rounded......................Detective Berry has demonstrated the ability to work well with others............Detective Berry has a very positive attitude...............

Sergeant Glade Austin

12

AN INVESTIGATOR'S NIGHTMARE

WAS IT MURDER by a prominent local citizen, or was it suicide? What should have been a professional death investigation turned into a mockery of the Lewis County Sheriff's Office's ability to conduct major investigations. Yet why was I surprised, when I had witnessed many other death investigations that were poorly investigated in my twelve year association with the Department?

The day started out like any other day; I dressed, had a cup of coffee, and went out to my unmarked police vehicle. I got into my car, started it, and while waiting for it to warm up, I checked to make sure my shotgun was free and accessible. I kept it in a soft case lying on the floor on the left side of the driver's seat. I turned on my police radio and signed into service at 8:00 a.m. I backed out of my driveway and started for my office at the County Courthouse. I had driven about two miles when I was contacted on the radio by Detective Steve Wilson. He told me he wanted me to respond to his location, giving me the address. Within a few minutes after signing off the radio, I got a call from the Chief Criminal Deputy on my Mobil phone. He said Detective Wilson was at the scene of what had been called in as a suicide. He told me that the husband of the victim had called in the suicide of his wife, but there were some circumstances that looked suspicious. He instructed me to look the scene over very carefully and determine if it was, in fact, a suicide.

Apparently the call had been dispatched as a possible suicide and Detective Wilson most likely assumed that was what he was responding to. Basically, I believe he started with a predisposed idea that a suicide had occurred.

About 30 minutes later I turned onto the rural road and went about one quarter of a mile when I saw a Lewis County patrol vehicle in the driveway. I recognized the blue Ford Taurus next to the patrol vehicle as the unmarked unit belonging to Detective Wilson. As I pulled into the driveway, I noticed the house appeared to be fairly new. It was a nice single story rambler that appeared to be well kept.

When I arrived at the residence, I checked my watch for the time and it was 8:20 a.m. I was greeted in the driveway by a Deputy. He was a veteran Deputy of the department and one that I respected. I had worked with him enough when I was a patrol deputy to know he was a good man. He had been the first arriving officer at the scene, and was the first person I wanted to talk to. I wanted to know what his observations had been when he first arrived. I wanted to know exactly what he had done, who he had talked to, and what he had heard. First observations at a crime scene are often critical. He said that the husband had told him that his wife had been upset about a pending divorce and that she had told him she was going to commit suicide. The husband told the Deputy that he had gone to bed with her around 10:00 p.m. the night before and had stayed awake until 5:00 a.m. He went to sleep after looking at the clock and awoke at 6:00 a.m. His wife was not in bed so he got up and looked around the house, eventually finding her in the bathroom closet. I took the information for what it was, second hand information.

The spouse and other family members are usually suspects in any suspicious death. This is the first place investigators start when conducting interviews.

By having the information given by the reporting party (person who called in the incident) before I went into the house, I would be able to see how well the information matched with what I observed. The Deputy told me that a friend of the victim had just left prior to my arrival. The friend had arrived to take her to the airport, apparently an arrangement that he and she had made the night before. I asked if anyone had obtained a statement from him and was told that Detective Wilson had taken one. The Deputy then advised me that the friend of the victim was a Sergeant with a Police Department near Seattle.

We then went into the residence and I was introduced to the husband of the victim. There were two other male subjects in the living room that I learned were the husband's co-workers. Detective Wilson came from a hallway and said he would show me where the body was. I told the husband that I would talk with him later, and turned to follow Detective Wilson.

When I entered the bedroom, I stopped to look around. I always tried to be as careful and as observant as possible when I entered a crime scene. Even though I knew several people had already been through the scene, I never took anything for granted. I looked at the bed which was to my left. The bed was positioned diagonally in the corner of the room with the foot of the bed facing the opposing corner. I saw that the bed frame was the type that had drawers for storage. I noticed that the blankets were turned down on the left side in a manner you would expect if someone had just gotten out of bed. The blankets on the right side were still up near the pillow. I looked closer and noticed that the blankets were not wrinkled or out of place on the right side, which suggested to me that the right side had not been slept in. On the right side of the bed next to the wall and toward the foot of the bed was a night-stand. I noticed a Black Velvet whiskey bottle that appeared to be empty sitting next to a lamp. As I stood in the doorway, continuing to take in the scene, I noticed there was a chest of drawers against the end wall to the right of the room. Its drawers were partially opened. A small TV sat on top of it along with numerous VCR tapes. A glass sliding door led out to a deck in the back yard.

Looking to the left again, I walked toward a doorway next to the night stand that led into the bathroom. I made a mental note to ask the husband which side of the bed he slept on and if his wife had consumed any alcohol the night before.

I stopped at the bathroom entrance and looked in, trying to pick up on anything that could be a clue to what happened during the hours before. On the wall to the right was a counter about 8 feet long. A large mirror covered the wall above the counter. On the mirror in large red print was the message, "I love you, please call me" and below that was the phone number, " XXX-123-XXX". I stood in front of the mirror and stared at the hand-written message. What was wrong with it? Hell, it wasn't a suicide note! And there was something else that seemed unique, the slant of the letters! I pointed it out to Detective Wilson, but I might as well have been talking to the wall. He wouldn't even comment on it. This would turn out to be the same response I got with the many other "red flags" that came up. He had responded to a report of a suicide, the husband said it was a suicide, and apparently he was going to accept it as a suicide! I asked Detective Wilson where the gun was that had been used. He told me he had removed it from the body for safety reasons and then proceeded to show me where he had found it. I wanted to ask him what he thought was going to happen if he had left the gun where it was. He was carrying his gun, and there were uniformed Deputies at the scene, so there were no safety issues. I asked Detective Wilson if there had been anyone else in the house besides the husband when the Deputy arrived. He told me that there had been three boys, the sons who had been present. I asked where they were, wanting to make sure we kept them separated from everyone else until they were interviewed. I didn't want any of them together or getting instructions from their father as to what to tell us. It was then that I learned that they were in the process of going out the door when the Deputy arrived. The Deputy had taken their names and let them leave, en-route to Olympia to their mother's.

I couldn't believe that potential witnesses had been allowed to leave before they were interviewed, not to mention letting them take a vehicle with them that may or may not have contained evidence. I commented about this to Detective Wilson, but he just went about his business, not responding one way or the other. This would turn out to be one of many mistakes that were made by officers who arrived at the scene that morning.

My frustrations were mounting as I mentally reviewed what I knew at this point. The gun had been removed from its original position, witnesses had been allowed to leave the scene, only one side of the bed appeared to have been slept in, the note on the mirror was not consistent with a typical suicide note, and the first arriving Detective was already willing to accept this as a suicide.

As I continued to look in the bathroom, I noticed a phone book on the counter that was opened to the Airlines section. Was she making plans to leave by plane? There was a phone on the counter nearby. I saw several gym type bags that were full of cosmetics, which appeared to be packed and ready to go. It was later confirmed that the victim had called and made reservations for a flight to Spokane. I took photos of everything and tried to conduct a thorough search. I looked for the lipstick tube that had been used to write the message on the mirror, but never found it. It would have been easy to recognize after being used as a writing instrument. Just to the left of the door leading into the closet where the body lay was a towel rack with a wash cloth on it. Upon closer examination I found that it had a few very small red stains on it. I collected it for evidence to be tested for blood. Thinking that it may have been used to clean up the crime scene, or to clean blood off the suspect, I then removed the sink drain "p-trap". I collected the water in the trap and later submitted it to the lab to be tested for blood samples.

I paused for a few moments and just stood there looking at the scene. I would do this at every crime scene I encountered, trying to replay in my mind the deadly scenario. I would try to visualize what may have occurred based on what was present at the scene and what the suspect and/or witnesses told me. There is another thing that any good cop will pay close attention to and it is known as a "gut feeling". Call it intuition, a sixth sense, insight or anything else you want, but it is a very real inner voice that has proven correct in more than one situation for Detectives around the world. We have all felt it at one time or another.

This was one of those times that my "inner voice" was screaming at me, "she did not kill herself!" I believed I was looking at a staged crime scene and was positive of it.

After I finished processing the bathroom, I proceeded to the closet where the body lay. The first thing that looked out of place to me was the victim's hair. The victim was lying on her left side, an electric blanket covering her. But the hair, it was swept upward and slightly to the back. There was a blood trail running downward from what appeared to be an entry wound just below and in front of the ear. Blood doesn't run uphill, yet her hair was saturated in blood and had the appearance of running upward. It also appeared that there was an unusually large amount of blood for a fatal head wound.

Detective Wilson told me that the husband had said that the pillow had been over his wife's head when he found her. Apparently, he said he had moved the pillow in order to check for a pulse on the carotid artery. I made a mental note to evaluate the position of the hair later. I took several photos, even though I knew that the Deputy and Detective Wilson had taken photos prior to my arrival.

I noticed a very pronounced impression of the gun barrel in the forehead area. Detective Wilson, in his ridiculous concern for safety, had removed the gun before the crime scene had been processed. I just didn't understand how the impression could have been so pronounced if the gun had been there for the short period of time that had been reported.

Detective Wilson told me he had removed the gun from near the left hand. I noticed that both her hands were under the electric blanket and that the blanket appeared to be grasped with her left hand. I thought this was a very difficult way to hold a weapon, with it being on the outside of the blanket. I then instructed the Deputy to ask the husband if his wife was left handed or right handed. The Deputy returned a few minutes later and told me that the husband had become very nervous when asked the question, and finally responded by saying that he didn't know.

Now the red flags were really waving. I knew that answer made no sense. What man or woman doesn't know the handiness of their mate? I then instructed the Deputy to go back into the living room and ask the husband if he was right handed or left handed. I wasn't that surprised when he returned and told me that the husband was left handed. My thoughts were that since I was right handed, wouldn't I be inclined to place something in a person's right hand? Wouldn't it be a subconscious, natural inclination for a left handed person to place the weapon in a left hand? Was that why he became so nervous when he was asked the question? It was just one more red flag that would be added to the growing list.

I noticed that the body was in a position that would prevent the closet door from being closed; her legs were in the way blocking the door. She was lying on her left side, legs slightly pulled up in somewhat of a semi-fetal position. Her left hand was near her forehead and her right hand was near her chest. This looked like a natural position when a person sleeps on their side. It was way too natural and I couldn't make it fit a suicide, no matter how I tried. I have seen a lot of suicides, but I have never seen one where the body was in such a natural position.

I found myself back in the bathroom just standing and looking at everything. I was missing something. I was sure of it, but couldn't see it. I just couldn't figure out what was eluding me.

I then stepped out into the hallway and called for the Coroner, using my handheld radio. This was one of the several mistakes I would make. Since Lewis County does not have a Medical Examiner, or

Chief Coroner that actually responds to major scenes, there was no need to have made the call so early. I wanted to get out of the scene for a few minutes for some fresh air, and then take a look at it again. I went into the living room where the men were talking. I told the husband that I had called for the Coroner and that it would be awhile before we were finished. I remember thinking, "he doesn't even have the compassion or decency to at least pretend he was sorry." His attitude and demeanor in itself was suspect in that he showed no signs of remorse and certainly no grief. I had been told by the Deputy that when the husband had called 911, he had sounded calm and did not seem to be excited at all.

I walked back into the bedroom and stood looking at the scene, again getting the feeling that I was missing something. I went to the right side of the bed, the side that did not appear to have been slept on. This was the side that we had been told the victim normally slept on. After a few minutes of looking at the bed, I went around to the left side. There were drawers built in the frame and I pulled out the one near the head of the bed. The drawer stuck and I had to pull hard to get it opened. It made a considerable amount of noise and due to the bed sitting diagonally in the corner; it would only open about half way before hitting the wall. Detective Wilson had said that the husband told him the gun that was used was kept in that particular drawer. There was nothing but clothing in the drawer so I turned my attention to the bottle of Black Velvet on the nightstand. It was empty so I went back out to the living room and asked the husband if his wife had drank anything the night before. He was quick to answer that she had drank about two shots from the Black Velvet bottle, holding up his left hand indicating about two inches with his thumb and first finger.

Detective Wilson left and I found myself alone to conduct the investigation. The Deputies who had been there when I arrived had left. I remember thinking, "where else in the world could a possible homicide be left to one man to investigate, but Lewis County?" But, I was used to working alone and put myself into the investigation to the best of my ability. But, as time went on it would prove that just my abilities alone were not good enough.

The Deputy Coroner arrived and I briefed her as to what I knew at this point. I then led her into the scene, explaining everything that had been done and what we had been told. I pointed out the message that had been left on the mirror and she immediately pointed out that it looked like the writing of a left handed person. She said she was left handed and recognized the left handed slant of the letters.

We went into the closet and I pointed to the position of the hair and told her about the gun being found on the outside of the blanket and the electric blanket. She was also concerned about these unexplained circumstances. She really became concerned when she checked the state of rigor mortis. Rigor starts at the feet and works its way to the upper body. After it becomes complete, it starts to rescind in the opposite direction. The entire process takes from 12 to 18 hours. If the victim had died at or near 5:00 am, as reported, the rigor would not have reached her upper body until somewhere around noon. Yet the body was in the early stages of completing its stiffening when I arrived at 8:20 a.m. This was physical evidence that didn't fit the story we were being told. The Deputy Coroner then checked the stage of lividity. This is done by pressing in on the body with one finger. The spot will turn white, just as it will if you press on yourself. If the color returns back to match the surrounding area, then lividity has not settled or become "fixed". In this case, the color didn't return, it stayed white. The blood had settled at the lowest points in the body and had become fixed. The problem we had is that it takes from 8 to 12 hours for lividity to reach the fixed stage. I knew the electric blanket could change the rate of decomposition in the body, but I didn't think it would change it to this degree in such a short time. I felt this was another piece of physical evidence that refuted the story we were being told.

The Deputy Coroner completed her portion of the investigation and called for the Mortuary to come pick up the body. She told me she would let me know when the autopsy would be performed, and I had worked with her long enough to know that she would call me.

A female arrived at the scene at about 9:30 a.m. She thought she was going to pick up the victim and take her to the airport. She said that she was the victim's best friend. During her statement, she was adamant that her friend never drank hard liquor and when she did drink, it was wine coolers. She said that her friend would never have committed suicide. She went on to say that her friend was always talking against suicide and that it was also against her religion. She said that her friend had been upset about her marriage breaking up, but certainly not enough to kill her self. She said that her friend was too strong of a person for that. There were no tears and no sign of emotional distress. It seemed like no one was grieving the sudden and unexpected death of the victim. Or was it unexpected?

I finished collecting, bagging and loading everything that I thought might be of some evidentiary value. I took one more look around and could not shake the feeling that I was overlooking something. I finally left, wondering why every death investigation in Lewis County had to be such a "cluster." This was not the way a professional homicide investigation was supposed to be conducted. In retrospect, I know that I made several mistakes myself that morning. I should have taken the mirror off the wall and every single item and fixture that was not nailed down. I should have taken the carpet from the closet. I should have attempted to get a search warrant and secured the entire house for a complete search. But the Deputy Coroner and I seemed to be the only ones who believed it to be a murder, and I didn't have any support.

I arrived at the evidence garage and spent the next few hours logging in everything I had collected. Items that needed to be sent to the State lab were packaged and made ready. The remainder was placed into our evidence storage.

I went upstairs to my office and made arrangements for the husband to come in for an interview. I had just gotten off the phone with him when it rang. It was the Deputy Coroner and she called to let me know the autopsy was scheduled for the next day at 2:00 p.m. I started to make notes in preparation for creating a timeline for the chain of events, according to the information I had so far. The phone rang again and when I picked it up, a female voice identified herself as the mother of the victim. She asked if I was the one investigating her daughter's death and I told her I was. "Can you tell me what happened?" she asked. She sounded very tired and the grief was apparent in the tone of her voice, yet, she had a strong voice, a matter-of-fact kind that goes straight to the issues. I knew instantly there would be no point in trying to soften the impact with passive answers. I have always believed that a victim's family has every right to know the truth, no matter what the truth may be. I also believe that a victim's family has the right to know what an investigation has produced, and to be kept apprised of any results.

I told her everything I knew at the time, and told her it was the general consensus at this time that her daughter had committed suicide. I wasn't about to elaborate on the concerns I had, or the mistakes that had been made. I was hoping to overshadow the mistakes with something positive before this was over. She asked if the husband's hands had been tested for gun powder. I told her they had not. She asked if the husband had been given a lie detector test and I told her that it was something that we were considering. She asked if the boys had been interviewed, and again I had to tell her they had not. She raised several more questions and I had to give her the same answers. God, she must think we are idiots! Then she dropped the "bombshell" question! "Detective Berry, do you think she committed suicide?" Crap! I was trying to stay away from that topic at this point in the investigation. I know it must have seemed like I paused for a long time before answering, but in reality, it was probably only a few seconds. I gave her the only answer I could. "There are a few things that concern me" and then I told her that I would rather talk to her in person. I asked if she was coming over and she said that she was. She asked what time I would be in my office the following day and I assured her that I would be in by 9:00 am. She said she would be there and the call was ended.

After I hung up the phone, I knew this lady was going to be a pain in the butt! She had a lot of questions and I knew she wasn't going to like the answers. She also had that direct, no nonsense approach that would not be pacified with half-truths and excuses.

I went back to my notes, a million things running through my mind, with none of them making any sense.

That afternoon, the husband came in as agreed. The following is what he told me: He said that on the day in question, he had been at his doctor in Olympia. He received a call on his cell phone from his wife and she was threatening to commit suicide. He said she was very distraught and he was concerned enough that he immediately started for home, keeping her on the phone until he reached the town they resided in. (This would have been about 30 to 40 minutes) He said that when he arrived in town, he stopped at the local hamburger place for a burger. After finishing his meal, he then went to the local school and watched a Christmas play. He stayed at the school after the play and helped close up before going home. He said that when he arrived home, his wife's friend was just leaving. He went into the house and his wife was still very upset and kept talking about killing herself. He said that before they went to bed, she had consumed some alcohol from the Black Velvet bottle that was on the night stand next to the bed. He held up his hand, indicating about 2 inches of liquor was in the bottle. After they went to bed, he kept her awake so she couldn't hurt herself. He said he never left her side. The last time he looked at the clock, it was 5:00 a.m., then the next thing he knew the alarm was going off at 6:00 a.m. She was not in bed so he got up and looked around the house for her. Not finding her, he went back into the bedroom and looked in their bathroom. He then said he opened the closet door and found that "she had committed suicide." He was adamant that the closet door was closed. He said he pulled the pillow off of her head and checked for a pulse on the right side of her neck. There was no pulse so he called 911.

[I ask the reader to pause for a few minutes and think about what you just read. What is your gut feeling at this point? How credible on face value, would you consider such a story? Is it perfectly believable or would you think it ludicrous?]

The next day, I met the Deputy Coroner at the Coroner's office at 1:30 p.m. I helped her get the body out of the cooler and placed on the stainless steel surgical table. I took the opportunity to take photographs and perform a cursory visual examination, making sure not to touch anything.

It was apparent that the victim had been very particular with her appearance. The fingernails were meticulously manicured. It made the badly torn nail on the middle finger of her left hand stand out like a beacon. The nail had been torn back into the quick and there was a hair like fiber lodged in the tear. This would have been a painful injury and not one that you expect a person so particular to leave unattended. This fit with the classical examples of a defense wound, which is a wound consistent with a struggle with her assailant.

When the Pathologist arrived, I briefed him on the circumstances and answered his questions before he began the autopsy. He took photographs at different intervals, as I did. The usual exterior examinations were performed, as well as the interior chest and stomach, including all organs. The most significant observable evidence so far was the torn fingernail and hair-like fiber.

The area around the head wound was cleaned and the hair shaved from the immediate area. At this point we could see that the hole just below and to the front of the right ear was the entry point of the bullet. Again photos were taken before proceeding. The interior examination of the skull cavity revealed that the bullet had passed through the brain stem, severing all the nerves. The bullet had come to rest, lodged in the left side of the skull.

As I went through the autopsy process, my mind was running like a video on fast replay. I kept seeing the body position at the scene, the hands under the blanket and the gun in her left hand. It sure didn't fit with the entry wound on the right side, plus she was right handed.

I asked the Pathologist if there would have been any body movement after the shot had been fired. He was adamant that she would have been immobilized instantly due to the brain stem having been severed; there would have been no movement at all. He stated that the body would have just gone limp. For me, this eliminated the idea that she shot herself and convulsive or reflex movements allowed her hands to get back under the blanket and in the position they were found.

Hair samples, swabs, nail clippings, blood, and clothing were collected and placed into the appropriate evidence storage.

I left the Coroner's office even more convinced that this was a murder, but at the same time I was unsure how I was going to prove it. When I got back to my office, I made notes to help me keep everything I did in the order that they occurred. As was typical for me, after everyone went home, I sat at my desk going over everything, making notes as I thought of things to follow up on, interviews that still needed to be done. I would spend hours working on flow charts, information sources, and time lines. Every witness interviewed would be added to the chart with notes for any follow up work needed. After I got the information we had so far in a somewhat organized fashion, I spent a couple of hours formulating a strategy for the interview with the husband the following day. Going into an interview without a specific plan and a memorized list of questions could mean the difference between success and failure.

If this was a murder and staged crime scene, then there were things that had to be considered for the right approach to the suspect. I had to consider that he was obviously more intelligent than the average "dirt bag," that we usually dealt with. If the scene had been staged, as I believed it had, then it would seem reasonable to believe the perpetrator had some knowledge of crime scene investigations. One could assume that anyone who knew the victim may have discussed crime scene techniques at some time. Most people have access to the internet and would know how to research information to find out what investigators look for. And the big question that needed to be answered was the electric blanket. Anyone could have easily found out that heat speeds up the decomposition process. There was no better way to prevent investigators from determining a close estimate of the time of death.

That was it! She had been killed much earlier than the time he said she shot herself. We had been told she shot herself between 5:00 a.m. and 6:00 a.m., yet there was some rigor starting when the first Detective arrived. Post-mortem lividity was fixed and rigor was pronounced when I arrived. Common sense should tell anyone that even with the electric blanket, the decomposition process couldn't have accelerated at that rate. I put the time of death around 1:00am to 2:00am.

Just before midnight, I decided to go home and try to get some sleep, even though I knew that was a dream in itself.

The next morning, I tried to brief the other Detectives as to my thoughts and what I considered was evidence. I might as well have been spitting in the wind, and it would have gotten greater results if I had. I then talked to my Sergeant and, as usual, I got nowhere. Later that morning, I overheard the one of the Detectives make the comment, "leave it to Jerry to try and make a murder out of a suicide." That was the only time I really wanted to kick his butt! I don't know who I despise the most, people who prey on and kill innocent victims, or lazy uncaring investigators who go through the motions, seeking the quick and easy closure of a case. It seemed like at every turn, I was met with either resistance or ridiculous comments. I felt like I was fighting two entities at the same time, the apathy of the Sheriff, and what I considered a dysfunctional Detective Division.

The Polygraph Examiner arrived and I gave him the needed information to administer the test to the husband. I had decided to let him take the polygraph test before any questioning. My thoughts were that if he failed, it would provide me with a great psychological advantage. The idea behind this was to hit him directly with an interrogation rather than an interview. The process took about 2 hours and when it was over, the Polygraph Examiner informed me that the results had been inconclusive. That simply means that he couldn't make a call one way or the other.

The husband was brought into the office and I tried the strategy

I had pre-planned. It didn't take long to realize that he appeared to me to be one cold individual! He showed no emotions at all, just like he did the morning we arrived at his house. None of the approaches were working and he was not responding. He sat in what I'm sure he thought was an appearance of relaxed posture. In reality, I noticed that it was more of an intentional consciously forced posture. He was rigid. His composure was forced. I'll give him credit, he was good, but then his freedom depended on it.

It was decided that his failure to pass the polygraph must have been due to the stress caused by the trauma he had experienced. He agreed that this must have been the case and agreed to wait a couple of days to recover and take the test again. I knew when he walked out of the office that we would never get another chance again, at least not when he was the most vulnerable.

To say I was disappointed would be an understatement. I was fighting apathy in the department, stupid comments, a Sergeant that was still operating in the 70's, and I had just watched my only chance at a confession walk out the door. That was the first time I thought about just letting it go, letting them close it as a suicide and to hell with them all. I even thought for a while that may be I "was trying to make it a murder." But the numerous inconsistencies and unanswered questions still had to be answered in a logical and common sense manner.

I tried to present everything I had accumulated to my Sergeant in a manner that would convince him that this was a special case; special in that it was possibly a staged crime scene and not something the County had any experience in. I tried to make him understand that we needed to work together to solve this, if it was ever going to be solved. But true to form, he kept telling me why it could be a suicide. He always called this "playing the devil's advocate". I wanted to ask him if he ever gave thought of "playing Detective" for once. He went so far as to tell me that I couldn't solve every murder and that I needed to "let it go", that some were "just going to fall through the cracks". I told him that I refused to conduct an investigation with that mindset, and that it was nothing more than self-defeating. I had my own thoughts about some falling through the cracks. May be some would, but I sure wasn't going to be a part of pushing them through.

Unless you have looked at the dead body of a murdered victim, you can't know the overpowering feeling that comes over you for the need to bring justice to them. You suddenly become their only hope, their only link to the truth. Death investigators have, or at least should have, a strong commitment to human decency and a feel a moral obligation to seek the truth. Sometimes doing the right thing can be the most difficult and can be the most costly. I knew that the right thing to do was continue to pursue this investigation, even if it went against the wishes of the Department.

Not surprisingly, the next day I got a call from the husband's attorney. He told me I was to have no more contact with his client and that all matters would have to be referred to him. Well, that pretty much shot any chances of getting any more out of the husband.

I still wanted to interview the three boys who had been in the house the night of the incident. I was still more than a little upset about them being allowed to leave the morning Deputies arrived at the scene. These were, at the very least, crucial witnesses, and would have been the most vulnerable to questioning the morning of the death. As I thought about it, the husband had been in control of the investigation from the time the first Deputy arrived at the residence. He had informed everyone it was suicide, using the very word when he called 911. It was he who made the decision that the only three witnesses would leave the scene before they were questioned. It was he who led the Detective through the scene, painting the picture of suicide that the Detective bought into.

I called him and let him know that I was not calling to talk to him about the investigation, but wanted him to bring his boys in for an interview. He told me that his boys were under the protection of his attorney and that he would have to consult with the attorney about them being interviewed. I asked him why he was concerned about his boys talking to me and he replied, "You might think that one of them is a suspect." I thought that was a weird answer and wondered what he meant. This really upset me because he was still controlling the investigation. I knew that he couldn't stop me from interviewing them and that his attorney even pretending to represent them would not only be unethical, but also a conflict of interest. My first thoughts were to go pick up the boys as material witnesses and bring them in, and to hell with the husband and his attorney. I told my Sergeant that I wanted to go pick up the boys, but he wasn't about to go for that and instructed me to just let the husband's attorney handle it.

That afternoon, I got a call from the attorney advising me that they would bring the boys in the following day and that he would be there to sit in on the interview. How stupid did he think I was? No way was he sitting in on what was basically a witness interview. But with absolutely no support or intervention from my supervisor, they got their way again. I remember how hopeless the investigation seemed, how defeated I felt at every turn.

My office partner was my only support base during this investigation and she thought from the first that it was murder. She was younger than my son, but had a natural propensity for investigative work. Lucy (not her real name) and I worked well together and she was always there as a sounding board for me. I always appreciated her feed back, as well as her woman's intuition. I asked her if she would be willing to sit in on the interviews with the boys and, as was always the case with her, she was quick to agree to help. I just wanted a witness of my own in the room and someone who would take notes.

The next day when the husband, his attorney, and the three boys showed up, I found it very hard to call up any enthusiasm for the pending interviews. By now the boys had probably and most likely, been well coached by the father. Any information we may have gotten from them the morning of the shooting, while they were still confused and scared, was gone now. I am sure the attorney had done his part, as well. It would be impossible to turn a fact finding interview into an accusatory interrogation with their attorney present. Any attorney worth anything at all would stop the interview at the first accusatory question by simply advising his client not to answer any more questions.

We decided to start with the youngest boy, who was 10 years old. He seemed to be honest with his answers and answered every question we presented to him. It was apparent that he did not have any information of any value. It was apparent that he didn't really like his stepmother that much, but as he told us, "never wanted anything bad to happen to her".

The next one who was 13 years old was a little different. For the most part, he seemed truthful enough and had very little information. Both boys claimed they never heard the gunshot, and neither had heard any fighting between their Dad and stepmother. He appeared, at times, to be a little evasive, but we couldn't tell if he was avoiding the answer or actually couldn't remember.

Then we got to the oldest. He was 17 and we knew that he had threatened to kill his stepmother a year prior. I have had enough interviewing and interrogation training to understand and recognize body language. A person will exhibit specific physiological reactions and postures that are indicative of either truthfulness or deception. The first thing he did when he sat down was extend his legs outward and fold his arms across his chest. This is a classic indicator that the person is hiding something. The extended legs are an attempt to put as much distance between the person and the interviewer. The folded arms indicates a "closed position," that is, an attempt to keep the truth from coming out; an attempt to close out the interviewer.

The interview did nothing but complicate the investigation. He just couldn't get his answers to come out the way he wanted. Most of his answers were either, "I don't remember", or "I don't know". My opinion was the little jerk was lying every time he opened his mouth. He gave me the impression that he was an angry young man whose problems probably ran deeper than just trying to protect someone.

I asked him if he saw his stepmother with a gun at any time during the evening before she died. He told us that he had been in his room lying on the bed with the door closed when his stepmother and her friend came in. He said that he had seen her friend hand her a handgun in a brown holster. I asked him where his stepmother and her friend had been standing when he saw the exchange of the gun. He said that she had been standing inside her bedroom and her friend had been standing in the hallway. I asked him how he had seen all this while lying on the bed with the door closed. He then said that he had been standing near the door to his room and the door was open at that time. I thought, "The stupid kid can't even keep his lies in order." I reminded him that he had just told me he had been lying on the bed with the door closed. He countered by stammering out, "I was at the door at first when I saw them, and then I closed the door." I asked him if he had ever threatened to kill his stepmother and he admitted that he "had once, but didn't mean it." The interview was little more than just going through the motions. The kids had several days to practice their stories. And the presence of the attorney in the room during the interview left little doubt how it would turn out.

From the very first day, I felt as if I was trying to run uphill with a great weight strapped to my back. I knew the answers were at the top, but I knew the weight would eventually keep me from getting there. The weight was the realization that the Deputy Coroner and I were the only ones who suspected this was a murder, and the knowledge that I was not going to get any help from the rest of the Department.

Just before Noon, the victim's mother arrived at my office, accompanied by her daughter's friend; the police offer. I introduced myself to both of them and invited them into the interview room. The male was a slender man of average height and had a quiet manner about him. He wore his light colored hair short, and had the look of a man who was dealing with his grief alone. The fatigue in his eyes could not hide the pain.

The mother was dressed in western cloths, much like you would expect from a horse breeder and trainer. She had the appearance of a strong individual, both physically and emotionally. Her face bore the lines that are common to those who have spent a life time working hard. She was clearly exhausted, the grief so obvious that it made me wonder how she was even able to talk to me this day.

Interviewing a deceased person's parents is one of the most difficult interviews. You know there are questions that you are going to ask that may upset the parent or bring out deep emotions. How do you confront someone who is suddenly faced with the death of their child, knowing they are going to expect you to have all the answers to their questions? I found that it was best to be completely honest and answer their questions. After all, they above all others deserve the truth. It is not the investigator's responsibility to determine what they are able to handle. If they didn't want the truth, they wouldn't ask. This is not to say that I believe they should be given every graphic, gory detail but, if asked for instance, where the bullet entered, tell them. A parent knows their child better that anyone, and can provide the most accurate profile of the victim.

The mother was probably the most level headed and realistic person I had ever interviewed who had suddenly had a loved one taken away. When she told me that she could accept her daughter committing suicide if we could prove it, I knew that she was only seeking the truth. She told me that her daughter had called her the night before and told her what flight and time she would be arriving in Spokane. She said that her daughter was looking forward to seeing her brother and grandmother. She told me about her daughter's fear of electric blankets and how they were so opposed to the idea of suicide because of their religious beliefs. She told me about how her daughter when upset, would go off into a closet or isolated corner of the house and curl up on the floor to sleep. The thing that stuck in my mind the most was how she described the plans her daughter had when she got to Spokane. She was going to get a job and start her life over, closer to her family.

It didn't take a rocket scientist to see that this lady had a very close relationship with her daughter. It was also obvious that she was no stranger to pain and the realities of life.

I watched her expressions as she talked about her daughter and tried to visualize what I would do in her position. I have a daughter about the same age as the victim. I couldn't even begin to understand how she must have felt, or how she was able to maintain any semblance of composure. I felt a sadness when she told me how she had gone to the airport and waited for her daughter to walk out of the jet way. What an empty and frightening feeling she must have felt when the last person came out, and her daughter was not there. And then to go back home and get a visit from the local Sheriff's Chaplain. When she answered the door and saw him there, I can only imagine what must have gone through her mind. Her iron will and constitution reinforced a belief that I have always held, and that is not everyone who gets depressed is suicidal.

I obtained a taped statement from her and got as much information about her daughter as I could. I wanted to build as much of a psychological profile of the victim as I possibly could. Knowing something about a person's habits, lifestyle, likes and dislikes, combined with the crime scene information, will often help the investigator reach logical conclusions as to what the person may have done.

After the taped interview was over, it was her turn to ask questions. She had been patient with me when I was the one asking for information, but it became apparent that her patience was running out. I had to try and explain why the boys had been allowed to leave the residence before any interviews were conducted. The best I could do was in telling her that they were gone before I arrived, and I was going to interview them at a later time. Then she wanted to know why the husband's hands had not been tested for gun powder residue. I told her that our Department had quit issuing GSR kits for field testing gun powder residue. I explained that according to my Sergeant the State Crime Labs were discontinuing these types of tests. She had several valid questions, none of which I could provide an acceptable answer for. She was perturbed, to say the least, and I felt like a fool as I tried to defend the first arriving Officers and their actions. Her last question to me that morning was, "Do you believe it was suicide?" She was looking straight into my eyes, and I knew she wanted my honest, personal opinion. I could only respond, "I have some concerns" and then I promised her that I would do everything in my power to find the truth. I also told her that she needed to prepare herself for the possibility of suicide, if that was my final conclusion.

The male with her was a Sergeant with another Police Department, and one of the victim's closest friends. He had arrived at the scene the morning of the shooting and had spoken with the Detective. He had been with the victim the evening before her death and was probably the last person outside her house to see her alive. I obtained a taped interview from him and he told me the following:

He said that he and the victim had once been involved in an intimate relationship and had always remained best friends. She had called him and told him about her husband wanting a divorce. He had driven down to Lewis County and met with her that afternoon. He said that he helped her pack some of her things and loaded them into her vehicle for her. They then went for a drive in his vehicle and talked about the impending divorce and things in general. She wanted him to pick her up the next morning and take her to the airport in Seattle. She had made plans to fly to her mother's.

He told me that she had called her husband from her cell phone while they were riding around, and talked for a few minutes. He said that she had never once mentioned suicide or even alluded to it during her conversation with her husband. He remembered the time of the call to be shortly after 5:00 pm, right after they left a local Mini Mart. He said that she was upset, but had plans and never once mentioned wanting to take her own life. He said that they drove around for awhile, just talking, and had stopped at the Mini Mart to get gas. He said he had bought the gas with a credit card and we should be able to verify that.

After the cell phone conversation, they drove back to her residence and he helped her load a few more things into her vehicle. He said that at one point, he had been standing in the hall at the entrance to her bedroom and she handed him a revolver in a brown holster. He asked her who it belonged to and she told him it was her husband's.

He said he told her that she didn't need to take anything that belonged to him and told her to leave it. She agreed and he unloaded the weapon and placed it in the drawer under the bed where she told him it was kept. After loading a few more things, they went for another drive. When they returned, her husband was just going into the house. He said she told him that she was going to stay the night and wanted him to pick her up at 5:00 am the next morning. He then left.

After the interview, I made notes for things to follow up on. One of them was to verify the time he bought gas at the Mini Mart. The other was to get the phone records for the victim's cell phone. I also needed to get the phone records for her mother's phone. These were all things that would verify times on the timelines chart.

Any times that can be verified are very important in establishing a timeline. That is, a verifiable record of times, places, and contacts where the victim and any suspects were during a 24 hour period prior to the incident.

Once a timeline has been established, the focus is concentrated on filling in the missing times. Suspects will usually give an accounting of their whereabouts during that 24 hour period. Then it is necessary to find out where they were during the time frame when the victim was killed. This is the time when most suspects will have a detailed explanation of where they were, but usually can't verify it with witnesses or receipts.

In every investigation, there are numerous questions that will come up, as well as numerous leads, some good and some false. Each question needs an answer, regardless of what it may be. Each and every lead needs to be followed to the end so there is nothing left to chance. I was faced with an apathetic Sergeant and a Sheriff's Administrative Team that had no interest in helping. The other Detective had made his decision that it was a suicide so he wasn't going to have any more to do with it. My Sergeant was so caught up in playing the "devil's advocate" that it seemed to me that he couldn't function outside of that mindset. I knew the importance of getting the answers before I could proceed, but no one else seemed to care one way or the other.

It was time to go through everything I had so far and try to make all the statements fit together in the timeline. It was time to list all the inconsistencies and issues of concern. Once the list was completed, then I would start at the top and work each one until a plausible answer could be given for each one. I would work through the list and the items that couldn't be answered would be added to a second list, which would be considerably smaller. The second list would be the focus point of the rest of the investigation.

The following is the first list that I put together outlining my concerns. I believed that each one needed an answer in order to successfully close the case.

1. Why did it take so long to call 911?
2. Why did the husband lie about the phone call on his cell phone?
3. Why was rigor so pronounced?
4. Why was lividity fixed?
5. Where was the holster to the gun?
6. Why was it that no one in the house heard the gunshot?
7. The husband did not know if his wife was right or left handed.
8. Why was the gun in her left hand, when she was right handed?
9. Why was the gun fired through the pillow?
10. Why was her hair swept upward?
11. Why did the husband say she had consumed alcohol?
12. Why the electric blanket when she was afraid of them?
13. The message on the mirror not being consistent with suicide.
14. Where was the lipstick tube that wrote the message?
15. Why was he trying to keep her awake instead of letting her sleep?
16. Why was the gun on the outside of the blanket?
17. We were told the closet door was closed, but we know it could not have been due to the position of the body.

I went to the funeral service that was held in Chehalis, WA. I usually attended the services of homicide victims in order to observe those who attended. It is not unusual to even video the proceedings. The tape can be reviewed later to see if there are any suspicious persons or circumstances at the services. My purpose was to watch for a suspect if he/she were there. I saw the husband in the appropriate location, the front row. What I didn't expect to see was his ex-wife.

She was sitting right there next to him, neither one of them were showing any signs of grief or remorse. I scanned the audience, but there was nothing unusual that I could see. When the services were over, I watched the ex-wife leave. I followed her out to the parking lot to get a description of the vehicle she left in.

I was able to recruit one of the Detectives to assist in some needed interviews. There were the co-workers and supervisors of the victim at Wal-Mart who needed to be interviewed. The personal things belonging to the victim had to be picked up from them and we needed to find out if they had any information at all that would help us. I asked the Detective to take care of these interviews and pick up the items belonging to the victim. I also assigned him the task of verifying any life insurance she may have had.

With the Detective taking care of these interviews, I made arrangements to meet with the victim's ex-husband. He was currently a Washington State Patrol Officer and lived in the Seattle area. He had been married to her for eight years and also knew the husband

I made the two and one half hour drive to his home. He told me that he had seen his ex-wife at her worst, but never heard her mention suicide, nor had he ever considered her suicidal. I asked him about her dislike for electric blankets. He said she was afraid of electric blankets and would not allow one on the bed. It was a surprise to him to hear that she had been found covered with one. When I asked if she had any peculiar habits, he told me that when she became upset, she would often go into a secluded area of the house and go to sleep on the floor. He said that he could see her going into the closet and going to sleep on the floor, especially if her husband came into the bedroom and had gotten into bed. He told me that she was stubborn and always had to have the last word and had to be in control. He didn't believe that she would have committed suicide and said that it would be more like her to make her husband pay one way or the other, than to take the easy way out. He said that he and she and been in a lot of disputes, and he reiterated that he had seen her at her lowest, and she never showed any signs of being suicidal.

After the interview, I took a statement from his present wife who had spoken to the victim on the phone the day before she died. This was basically another way to lock down and verify times in the time line I was working on. She didn't have any information that I didn't already have.

When I got back to my office, I placed a call to Rod Englert, a well known forensic expert in the field of blood spatter interpretation and crime scene re-construction. He had been involved with the O.J. Simpson case and was well received in the law enforcement community throughout the United States. He resides in Portland, Oregon and it would be a one day event for us to have him look at a few things. I wanted his opinion on the blood flow pattern on the victim's neck and head. I was hoping he could provide an answer to the appearance of the blood having run up into her hair.

Rod agreed to look at the photos (at a nominal fee of $600.00 an hour) and asked if I could bring the weapon that had been used, as well as the pillow and blanket. "I'll bring everything we have if you want it, I replied". I told him that I would talk to my Sergeant and get back with him. When I approached my Sergeant with the request, I was surprised that he agreed, even agreeing to go with me. I called Rod back and made an appointment for the following week. I was determined to get as many of the "red flag" questions answered as I could.

We left the office shortly after 9:00 a.m., the requested evidence loaded in the vehicle, with high hopes of getting some answers from Rod Englert. When we arrived at Rod's residence, I said, "at $600.00 an hour, no wonder he lives in a place like this." The home was beautiful, complete with a guesthouse and separate office where we were led by Rod. For the next two hours I answered questions and watched Rod as he took several photographs of the gun. He had some very expensive photography equipment and produced some very high resolution photographs. He examined the blanket and pillow, paying extra attention to the area where the bullet passed through.

When he was done, my Sergeant asked him if he thought it was a suicide. "I would say that there is a 75% chance that it would be possible for her to have shot herself," he said.

At no time did he ever say that it was his opinion that she committed suicide. On the way back to Chehalis, I realized that we had just spent $1,200.00 for a few high quality photographs of evidence we already had.

As it turned out, we never received an official report from Rod Englert; nothing to place in the case file. He never gave an opinion on the blood pattern that I felt was so important. Blood pattern interpretation was his expertise and the primary reason I contacted him, and it turned out to be the one thing I didn't get. For the next several weeks I struggled with the investigation. Every time I tried to talk to my Sergeant, he always had an answer for every concern I had. The total lack of emotion by the husband the morning he called 911 was accepted as, "maybe he was glad she was gone, you can't make someone love their spouse." The stops the husband made on the way home the evening she allegedly called him threatening suicide; the hamburger, and the school play - they were explained as, "maybe he is just an insensitive bastard." And the missing lipstick tube and message on the mirror? "Maybe she got rid of it and wanted to make us think someone had killed her." It was like that with every single concern. Then he would always finish with, "I'm just playing devil's advocate." God, how I've come to hate that phrase!

This was the first time that I became acutely aware of my own inexperience and training in homicide investigations. There were so many things that should have been done in the beginning, and so many things that probably could still be done. I would lie awake at night, trying to come up with something that would turn this case around. I played every possible scenario I could come up with. It always came back to murder.

Over the next several weeks, I received several calls from Police Officers around the West Coast who had known the victim. They were all adamant that she would not have committed suicide. They all commented on how stubborn she was and how strong she was. They all agreed that suicide was not part of her being. Even with all the calls, none of them gave proof or evidence regarding the event at the victim's house on that fateful morning.

A few months later, I received a letter from the husband's attorney, basically advising us that if we didn't close the case, he would take steps to get it closed. When I read the part insisting that we close the case or he would take steps to close it, I got mad! I went into my Sergeant's office and showed him the letter. "Who does this guy think he is, ordering us to close the case?" "I'll close it when I'm done and he can go to hell," I said. My sergeant's only response was to say, "He can't tell us when to close it." "Leave it here with me and I'll take care of it" he said. Maybe he will do something to help me after all, I thought. I thanked him and headed home.

The next day I woke up with a sore throat and a bad cough. Even though it was Friday, I stayed home. I knew that it would take a couple of days before the cough would go away and I could return to work. When I get sick, it always starts the same way, so I know what I need to do for the first two days. I spent the weekend in bed, but when Monday rolled around, I was in my car and headed for my office. If I had known what I was going to find when I got there, I might have stayed home for several more days.

When I got to my office, I noticed that the case file was on my desk. I kept it on the shelf, so I knew that someone had moved it. It was opened to the section where my Sergeant's statements were. Every person interviewed and every Officer who writes a report has a section that is divided and tabbed with their name for quick access. The first thing I saw was a copy of a letter my Sergeant had written in response to the letter the attorney had sent. I couldn't believe what I was reading. I remember jumping up from my chair and yelling, "He can't do this!" I'm the one who decides when we close the case." I couldn't believe that my Sergeant had succumbed to the attorney's threats. He didn't have the courage to tell the attorney that the Sheriff's Office would decide when the case would be closed. He took the easy way out. I went straight to him and asked him what was going on. He told me that based on "the totality of circumstances," he believed that the investigation was completed and warranted being cleared as a suicide. Totality of Circumstances was another one of his favorites that I hated.

Supplemental Report by (the sergeant)
May 26, 1999
Incident Type: Death Investigation/Suicide

Item # 8: On 05/26/99 at approximately 1030 hours, I, _____, Detective Sergeant, Lewis County Sheriff's Office talked with (name removed) of the Attorney General's Office H.I.T.S. Program in regards to this case. This conversation took place at the end of the weekly Detective meeting in Centralia.

He advised me that he and his colleague, (name removed), also with the H.I.T.S. program and reviewed our case file and the photographs and based on the totality of the information available at this time, they were both in agreement that they felt that this was likely a suicide. With the additional test results showing some chemicals from the firing of a handgun on her hands and after hav-

ing this case also reviewed by Rod Englert, a national expert on death reconstruction and his opinion being also that this was a suicide, it would be appropriate at this time, based on the totality of the information that this case be closed exceptionally and that the death be ruled as suicide. This would not preclude the case being re-opened if significant information should come before us at a later date indicating otherwise.

Detective Sergeant _____, # 2D1
Lewis County Sheriff's Office

I walked out of his office feeling defeated and alone. It was that day that I lost all respect for my Sergeant. Up to that point, I still liked him in spite of the poor quality investigations that he led. I went back into my office and slumped into my chair. The longer I sat there the madder I got, and it was anger that would keep me going for the next four years. I immediately wrote a supplemental report stating my objections to my Sergeant closing the investigation as a suicide. I then placed it into the case file so it would become a permanent record.

Supplemental Report
Det. Berry
Incident Type: Suspicious Death

Item # 8: On 05-28-99, I Detective Berry, found a copy of a follow up report submitted by Detective Sergeant _____ reference this case. Detective _____ had advised me he had talked to (name removed) of the Attorney General's Office on Wednesday and (name removed) told him they would lean towards this case being a suicide case based on reading the report and viewing the photographs. It is the opinion of Detective Sergeant _____ that this case be closed and ruled a suicide at this time.

However, as the primary investigating officer, I do not agree with this conclusion and at this time I still do not believe this was a suicide. I base my opinion on the fact that those experts which have reviewed this case have only looked at the photographs and the case report. They have not had close contact with the suspect in this case nor have any of them been directly involved with this investigation. There is an incredibly large amount of inconsistencies and *circumstantial evidence that I feel make it impossible to rule this case as a suicide at this time.*

Therefore, as the primary investigating officer, the best I can do is to express my concern and opinion and to suspend this case until further information is developed. I do not recommend this case be cleared as a suicide.

Detective J.C. Berry #2D6
Lewis County Sheriff's Office

The report my Sergeant had submitted was basically a false report. It was false because he stated that the employees of the Attorney General's Office had reviewed the case file and photographs, when in reality they had only been provided a synopsis of the investigation and only a few photographs. It was false because he stated that Ron Englert had said it was his opinion it was suicide, when in reality Mr. Englert never made such a statement. It was false because he stated the lab results showed chemicals from the firing of the gun, when the lab actually stated that the traces were so miniscule, that if they had to testify, they would testify to no significant traces found.

The weeks tuned into months with no break in the investigation. Everyone seemed to have forgotten about the death of this young female; everyone except her mother who would not let it go. I would receive a call from her at least once every month, asking what I was doing on the case. She would have various questions about the evidence, insurance claims, and direct questions about persons she thought needed to be interviewed. I always dreaded the calls, knowing what she was going to ask and not having any answers for her. I believed it was murder and she believed it was murder. Up to this point, I had only told her that there were some inconsistencies that concerned me, and that I was trying to get answers to them. But eventually I decided to tell her what my opinions really were about her daughter's death, and where the investigation had stopped. She at least had the right to know the truth, and I was running out of excuses when she called.

I called her and made arrangements to meet with her in Centralia on the following evening. She wanted to know if I had found something, so I told her that I thought her daughter had been murdered. She asked if she could bring her daughter's best friend with her and I told her it was fine with me.

I met with her and her daughter's friend the next night at about 8:00pm at Shari's Restaurant. I told them what my observations had been when I arrived at the scene on the morning of the incident. I explained the course of the investigation and how it came to be closed as a suicide. She was stunned to find out that I had believed it was murder from the beginning and that no one was going to do anything about it. It was one of the most difficult conversations I had ever had with a victim's family. I made another promise to her that night, and it was that I would do everything I could to find the truth and to not let the case go.

Letter From Chief Deputy Doench
October 27, 1999

Dear Detective Berry:

Your assignment as a Detective has been reviewed for the January 3, 2000 shift change. I have discussed this with your supervisor, the Sheriff, and I have reviewed your letter of interest where you indicate you wish to remain in the Detective Division. I have decided to continue your assignment as a Detective for another year. I will reassess your assignment in October of 2000.

Your performance in the Detective Division has met all expectations and the comments from your supervisor and coworkers have been extremely favorable. You have represented the Sheriff's Office well and I am happy to have you continue in this assignment.

Sincerely,

Joseph A. Doench, Chief Criminal Deputy.

As time went on, this case became low priority and all but forgotten. Every time I would bring it up to my Sergeant, I was brushed off or told the case was closed. In July, 1999, I asked my Sergeant if I could take the case file to a homicide class that I was scheduled to attend in Seattle. "No. All you will get is another opinion, and we don't need more opinions," was his reply. In September 2000, I contacted Vernon Geberth, a nationally known expert in homicide investigations. I had been to one of his three-day seminars, and was impressed with his knowledge and background. My Sergeant had been to one of Vernon's seminars and had insisted I go. Vernon retired from the New York Bronx Police Department as the Commander of the Homicide Division. He is the author of the book, *"Practical Homicide Investigations and Techniques"* The book is used by police agencies throughout the world and is referred to by many, as the "bible of homicide investigations."

I went to my Sergeant and asked him if I could have Vernon review the case file. He still would not consent to an outside review, even by someone as well respected as Vernon Geberth. His reasoning was the same, "we don't need more opinions." "Damn it we do need expert opinions," I replied. But it was to no avail; I couldn't get him to agree to let me contact Vernon.

The next person I contacted was Gary Ashenbaugh, another expert, in the field of S.C.A.N. Scientific Content Analysis is a system that was created in Israel. It is a method of deception detection by analyzing a person's statements. It is a very complex system and would require a book in itself to explain how it works. Gary Ashenbaugh agreed to analyze the statement I had taken from the victim's husband. I sent him a copy and three weeks later I received a response from him. He gave a brief summary of his analysis, concluding that the husband had been deceptive during the interview. He closed the summary recommending that we not rule the death a suicide. A complete report with investigative recommendations would be forwarded for the price of $375.00. This seemed like a great price after what Rod Englert had charged us, and we would be supplied a written report.

I had requested the analysis without my Sergeant's knowledge, but I had to get his approval before I ordered the report. I contacted him and provided the information, showing him the summary supplied by Gary Ashenbaugh. Much to my dismay, he denied me the request to order the report. He "didn't want to spend any more money on the case." I thought that we might be making a little progress with Gary Ashenbaugh's report and if enough experts agreed it was not a suicide, then maybe the Department would be more inclined to reopen the investigation. I couldn't figure it out. Were they denying me because of personal reasons, or were they really just stupid?

In November 2000, the annual meeting of the Washington Violent

Crimes Investigators Association was scheduled to meet on the 23rd. I had joined the Association the first year it was formed and was the only member from Lewis County. I told my Sergeant about it and requested to be allowed to attend. I also requested to be allowed to take this case file with me for review. My thought was to have a group of experienced investigators review the file, give me an opinion, and possibly suggestions on how to solve it. My request was made through the usual process by submitting a training request form to my Sergeant.

A few days later, he called me and told me to meet him in the Chief Criminal Deputy's office. I wondered what this was all about. When I walked in, my Sergeant said, "I've got some good news and some bad news." The good news is your request to attend the W.V.C.I.A. meeting has been approved, and I'm going with you." "The bad news is that you are not going to take the case file with you." It had become apparent to me that they were not going to allow this murder to be solved. I walked out of the office defeated again and wondered why they were so hell bent on not getting the answers to this case.

What the Department didn't seem to understand was that I was a part of the Department, and the Department's reputation was my concern as well. I worked very hard to make sure that I did the best job I could do. I had always tried to represent the Department in a manner that would represent the Sheriff and the Department as a professional organization. However, it seemed to be a near impossible task.

I contacted the mother of the victim and told her that there was nothing else I could do and that every request I had made for an outside review had been denied. She asked for the names of those experts I had contacted so I gave her the names of Geberth and Ashenbaugh. She said she was going to request a copy of the case file and would try to get it reviewed by Geberth herself.

After so much stonewalling, I began to find that I was becoming more and more frustrated. I started to resent the Sheriff and his Administration for not working to solve the case. I began to resent my Sergeant and the Detective who first responded to the scene. My frustrations began to manifest itself in my daily attitude toward my work, as well as toward my motivation to do a good job. This started a chain reaction of events that only made my life more miserable. I felt like the administration began to target me, looking for any excuse to call me in for a verbal reprimand. Suddenly I went from an excellent and praised employee to one who couldn't even submit a report without it being found faulty. One misspelled word, one block that wasn't checked, and it would be enough to be called in for what they like to call a "consultation". One day, while handcuffing a suspect, a large red rooster attacked my right leg. The two inch long spurs penetrated about 1/2 inch into my leg just below the knee. Chickens are not the cleanest, so after dropping off the prisoner I notified dispatch that I was going to be at the hospital for a tetanus shot. Even though I announced over the radio where I was, I was subjected to one of their counseling sessions because I failed to make personal notification to my immediate supervisor that I had been injured. It didn't matter that I came straight to the office after getting the tetanus shot, and filled out the appropriate paperwork. They must have been crazy if they thought I was going to place some petty little protocol before my own health and safety. Day in and day out this would occur.

This was a common practice of the Undersheriff and Chief Criminal Deputy. They loved manipulating employees and once a Deputy became their target, they made that person's life a living hell. Their tactics were nothing less than harassment and were instrumental in the Department loosing over 60 deputies in less than six years. Only those who were within a couple years of retirement, or those who were financially trapped, stayed on. It was my opinion the young Deputies who had no life experiences were easily intimidated, and were able to be molded by the bastardized system of administration put into place by the Sheriff.

It took the mother a long time and several letters to the Sheriff before he finally agreed to allow Vernon Geberth to review the case file. The case file and photos were sent to Geberth. She ordered the report from Ashenbaugh, having to pay for it herself. The more pressure she put on the Sheriff's Office, the more pressure they put on me. The Chief Criminal Deputy called me into his office and told me that he had reconsidered and sent the file to Geberth. "What a liar," I thought. He didn't have a damn thing to do with it; it was the mother's persistence and constant pressure on the Sheriff that got the file to Geberth. He wanted to know if I had been giving information to the mother and I told him I gave her answers to her questions when I could. As it turned out, he would spend a lot of time trying to find out if I had "given information" to anyone about the investigation.

It was a clear sign to me that he knew the investigation was screwed up and none of them knew how to make it right, so they were trying to keep it under wraps. Why couldn't they just step up to the plate and admit their mistakes, then do everything they could to make it right? Did the Sheriff and his team lack the skill, knowledge or the guts to do the right thing? It was so bizarre that I never figured it out.

A few days later the Chief Deputy called me into his office and he was obviously upset. "I got the report back from Vernon Geberth, and he makes us look like the Keystone Cops". "Gee, I wonder why," I thought. He wanted to know what I had told Vernon. I knew what he was getting at and I knew he was looking for a way to blame me for Vernon's analysis. He didn't know that I knew he had requested only a "verbal report" from Vernon. With only a phone call from Vernon, he could say anything he wanted and deny anything Vernon told him. But now he had an unexpected official report that would have to become a part of the case file. "From now on, I am the lead investigator on this case; you will do nothing else with it." "No problem" I said. He was finding himself being backed into a corner and he didn't like it. He then told me that he was going to set up a meeting with everyone who had been involved in the investigation and "go over Vernon's report."

I called the victim's mother and told her that the Department had received Vernon's report and they were not happy. She told me that she had sent a letter to Sheriff McCroskey, asking for answers to numerous questions. He had not responded the first time she sent the letter, so she sent the second one certified, requesting a signature of receipt. She was having great difficulty getting the Sheriff to respond to her, and getting him to provide any answers.

The reason I think the Sheriff could never respond to issues was simple; he never really knew what went on in the Department. He was always too busy running around playing the politician. He had us (the Detectives) provide him with the status of investigations just prior to a news release or public meeting, yet when he spoke to the citizens, it sounded like he was actually involved. I think we could have fed him any kind of crap and he would have repeated it to the public. He was that dependent on us to provide him with the right things to say involving any major investigation.

The Sheriff and his Administration now had three major setbacks now with reports from three experts.

This is Vernon's report that was sent to the Sheriff.

VERNON J. GEBERTH, M.S., M.P.S., BBA, FBINA

(Name removed), Female White, 33 years of age d/o/b 9/16/65
Private Residence at (Address removed)
CRIME SCENE

On December 16, 1998 sheriff's deputies were dispatched to the above address to investigate what was described as a possible suicide involving a gunshot wound to the victim. The first deputy to arrive was Deputy -------
----, who was met by the husband of the deceased. The husband's name is (name withheld). He had three young boys with him in the hallway of the home and he advised the deputy that he was sending them to his ex-wife's house. Mr. (name removed) then directed Deputy ---------- to the master bedroom and then into the bathroom area. The deputy reported that he observed a female subject lying on the floor on her left side with a .32 caliber pistol lying next to her forehead. He observed that she had blood in her ear region and on her lower jaw area. The officer also noted that she was in her pajamas and had an electric blanket covering her body. The officer noted that the electric blanket was turned on. The deputy asked one of the First Aid crew that had responded to have someone examine in the victim and it was confirmed that the victim was in fact dead. It is not known if the Emergency Responders were at the scene before the deputy. The deputy directed that the crime scene be maintained and he requested Detective assistance. Deputy ----------asked (name removed) what had transpired. Mr. (name removed) advised the deputy that he and his wife were having some marital problems and they were planning on separating. He stated this his wife told him she was thinking about suicide. He stated that he persuaded her to stay at the residence and they had been talking until he fell asleep about 5:00 A.M. When the alarm clock woke him up about 6:00 A.M. he discovered his wife shot and called 9-1-1.

OBSERVATIONS

Detective Jerry Berry was requested by Chief Criminal Deputy ----------
--- to respond and assigned him to investigate the death. Detective Berry observed that the victim was lying on the floor of the walk-in closet in the bathroom. The victim's body was partially covered with an electric

blanket, which was plugged into a receptacle in the bathroom and was still on. Deputy --------- reported that the weapon, which had been removed by Detective ---------, was recovered in the victim's left hand. The blanket covered the left hand and the gun was in the blanket. Detective --------- advised Detective Berry that he had removed the gun from near her head but had taken several photos before doing so. He pointed out the impression the gun had left on the side of the victim's head where it had been lying. Detective Berry noticed that the victim's hair was in what appeared to be an unusual position. It was swept back and upward. Also, it was Detective Berry's opinion that the impression of the gun on the victim's head was quite pronounced indicating that it had been there for some time. The husband stated that this even occurred sometime between 5:00 A.M. when he fell asleep and 6:00 A.M. when he discovered his wife's body.

The blanket, which covered the deceased, was over her left hand and that her left hand was closest to the gun. When Detective Berry attempted to pull the blanket back for a closer examination he discovered that the blanket was in her hand and there appeared to be some rigor mortis to her limbs.

Detective Berry also took note of some writing on the bathroom mirror, which appeared to have been written in red lipstick. It said, "I love you." "Please call me." Along with a telephone number which was later determined to be the victim's grandmother.

When the Deputy Coroner arrived, Detective Berry requested her to examine the body for rigor and lividity. The coroner indicated that there was fixed lividity in the stomach area. She also indicated that there was possibly more rigor than would normally be found if the deceased had only been dead since 6:00 A.M.

Detective Berry also made several other observations of the bed in the master bedroom, the empty liquor bottle and the lettering on the mirror. Detective Berry re-interviewed (name removed). After this interview Detective Berry had some concerns about his apparent lack of remorse as well as the many inconsistencies in his statements coupled with the observations he had made at the crime scene.

REVIEW AND ANALYSIS OF MATERIALS

The undersigned reviewed a number of reports and some crime scene photographs that were provided to me for an investigative analysis and assessment. The time of death was determined to have been between 5:00 A.M. and 6:00 A.M. according to the reporting witness, who was the husband of the victim. ------, who by all accounts was a very light sleeper, stated that he never heard the sound of the gunshot. Yet he was in the next room. According to other interviews conducted by Detective Berry, (name removed) would awaken at the slightest sound and had in the past chastised his wife about her dogs coming onto the bed and disturbing him.

I also found it interesting that friends of deceased stated she hardly ever drank hard liquor but would drink wine coolers. (name removed) stated that his wife had consumed the liquor in the empty Black Velvet bottle. However, toxicology indicated that there was no alcohol in her system.

According to (name removed) original statement he didn't know if his wife was left handed or right handed. **I find this to be absolutely incredulous. I think that most reasonable persons would agree that a spouse knows the handedness of the other spouse.** (name removed) demeanor from the time of the report and throughout the investigation is one of total unconcern. His lack of remorse speaks volumes. In fact, when (deceased's friend) called the residence on the morning of December 16 expecting to speak to (deceased) regarding taking her to the airport, he got Mr. (name removed) on the phone who told him that (deceased)had committed suicide. According to (deceased's friend) Mr. (name removed) made this comment matter of factly and did not show any emotion.

The gun that fired the shot into (victim's) head belonged to Mr. (name removed) who stated that he thought that her friend had taken the gun so that she wouldn't use it on herself. Later on this information provided by Mr. (victim's friend) proved to be untrue. Actually, while assisting (victim) in removing her belongings she showed (him) the gun. He had advised her not to take the gun since it belonged to Mr. (name removed) He unloaded it and put the gun in a drawer under the bed on the left side where Mr. (Name removed(always kept it. According to (friend) *There was never ever any conversation between him and (deceased) about her using the gun to commit suicide.*

The electric blanket, which covered deceased's body, poses and interesting question. Everyone who was interviewed stated that deceased did not like electric blankets. Her former husband, her boyfriend and others stated that she would not use an electric blanket and when she spent time with her boyfriend, who had an electric blanket on his bed, she insisted that it not be turned on.

Did the offender believe that the heat from the electric blanket would make the death appear to be more recent? The actual time of death was reported to be between 5:00 A.M. and 6:00 A.M. **Was deceased actually killed earlier? It is apparent that whoever killed deceased needed enough time to stage the scene and present a scenario that might be construed to be a suicide.** However, the fixed lividity and the on-set of rigor are postmortem changes that conflict with reported time of death. Likewise the postmortem artifact of the impression of the revolver on the victim's head would have taken a longer period of time to produce. Mr. (name removed) stated that he went to bed with his wife at 10:00 P.M. and never left her alone until he fell asleep at 5:00 A.M. Mr. (name removed) even stated to Detective Berry that deceased had pleaded with him to make love to her and Mr. (name removed) stated, "that did happen." Yet, the observation of the bed by Detective Berry indicates that only one person was in the bed. Also witness statements and telephone records indicate that deceased was alone and talking to friends until 12:45 A.M. It was during those telephone calls that she confirmed her pick-up for the airport and according to (friend) seemed happy to be going to Spokane. My impressions of deceased is that she took pride in her appearance and certainly, according to friends that were interviewed, would not have tolerated a broken fingernail.

Her best friend (female), stated to Detective Berry that victim had informed her that Mr. (name removed) had told deceased that he wanted a divorce and was going to go back to his ex-wife. Friend stated that deceased was upset about this but certainly wouldn't consider killing herself. In fact, she had discussed her plan on moving to Spokane.

Another Female, another person close to deceased stated that deceased had never mentioned suicide. Ms. (name removed) stated, "This woman loved life and she was very meticulous about herself and about her health and being fit." Her ex-husband, who is a trooper for the Washington State Patrol and been married to deceased while she was in the Washington State Patrol. He stated they had been married for about eight years and had problems that were most financial. He stated he had seen her at her worst but would never even consider her to be suicidal. He stated she was very headstrong and liked to be in control.

More importantly, I don't believe she ever would have shot herself in the head. Deceased had spent nearly $20,000 on her teeth and was keenly aware of her looks and appearance.

The gun had no fingerprints, which is not surprising if someone had taken the time to wipe it clean. The gunshot residue testing on deceased's hands were inconclusive.

The second finger on her left hand had a badly torn fingernail and injury. There was a hair like fiber stuck in this torn nail, which would seem more like an injury suffered during a struggle and would explain the transfer of evidence to the victim.

In my opinion the crime scene was staged. The writing on the mirror in lipstick is over dramatic and unnecessary. The comparison of deceased's writing on a Birthday card did not match the writing style of the alleged suicide note. **Even the message doesn't make any sense whatsoever. Why leave a note for your grandmother to call you if you are going to kill yourself?**

There was a delay in notifying the police. Mr. (name removed) stated he discovered his wife's body at 6:00 A.M. Yet he doesn't call for twenty minutes. When the police arrive he is cool, calm and collected.

Early on in this investigation the police had an opportunity to confront the husband with the number of inconsistencies as well as gain access to his children, who were certainly old enough to be questioned. However, there was a lack of apparent coordination between the patrol deputy and the first investigator, who seemingly was going along with the suicide theory until the arrival of Detective Berry who began to ask some hard questions.

The first officer did not follow standard death investigation procedures in detaining everyone who had been present when the death was discovered. The husband and his three children should have been detained by the officer pending arrival of the investigators who would have been able to interview these witnesses and ascertain what had transpired prior to their arrival. No one should have been allowed to leave and all of the vehicles should have been examined.

As a result valuable information was lost during this preliminary inquiry. The crime scene was obviously not protected from the onset. It was the husband who was directing the deputy through the scene. Also, it isn't clear to the consultant from the reports as to how many emergency responders were in the scene and had access to the scene.
----------------, who was the first Detective to respond, apparently

"bought-in" to the suicide theory early on. He seemingly accepted the premise that the victim had taken her own life based on the husband's explanation of marital difficulties as the cause for the victim's despondency. His preliminary examination of the body was done perfunctorily with an eye towards a quick resolution of the case. His disturbance of the evidence in the scene prior to the arrival of Detective Berry compromised the entire investigation.

OPINION

In my professional opinion, Deceased was the victim of a Homicide. She did not commit suicide as reported by her husband. Deceased did not fit any "Suicide Profile" that I'm familiar with. In fact, only her husband contends that she committed suicide. Everyone else, who was interviewed, stated emphatically that this could not be the case. Those who were close to deceased are adamant that she was not suicidal, loved life and would never consider killing herself.

She had made both short and long term plans. The evening before her death she had made airline reservations. Her best friend and former boyfriend, a Sergeant in the (withheld), WA Police Department, had helped her pack her belongings. She originally was going to leave but her husband convinced her to stay the evening. He helped her move her belongings from his truck to her car. Later that evening, she had called hem around midnight. She had seemed calm and had a definite plan of action, which was for him to pick her up and bring her to the airport.

According to her friends she was upset that her marriage was over. However, at no time in her conversation with these friends did she indicate that she was contemplating taking her own life. The only person who states that she was suicidal was her husband, whose gun was used and who discovered her body.

The facts and circumstances of her death are high suspicious and not consistent with suicide cases the consultant has reviewed. There were many inconsistent statements made by her husband that the police were not able to pursue. Furthermore, his total lack of concern and remorse throughout this investigation are troublesome and raise the level of suspicion as to his involvement in his wife's death.

Date: 11/27/00   Vernon J. Geberth, M.S., M.P.S.
                         HOMICIDE AND FORENSIC

CONSULTANT

Along with Vernon's report, was a report by Raymond Pierce, from whom Vernon had requested an independent review. His conclusion was that the case should not be closed as a suicide. This is his report.

RMP INTERNATIONAL
ADVANCED INVESTIGATIVE CONSULTATION AND TRAINING

November 21, 2000

Vernon Geberth
PHI Investigative Consl., Inc.
PO Box 197
Garnerville, NY 10923

Dear Vern:

I've reviewed the case material you forwarded from the death investigation of (name removed). I've attached a series of questions for Det. Berry that may assist him in adding a few more inconsistencies to his lengthy list.

An investigative point that may have been identified earlier in the investigation, but not included in the case materials sent to you, could be very important in supporting the circumstantial evidence that Deceased was in fact the victim of a homicide. The two crime scene photographs of the bathroom mirror can be used as a strong indicator of the approximate height of the offender who printed the three-line message. If the height of the first line of the message wasn't measured from the bathroom floor, it can be approximated to the inch by identifying the doorway height and the height of the crime scene investigator in the photograph.

When a burglar disables an outside utility line, before entering a building, the cut is almost always made at eye level. When the average person is given a piece of chalk and asked to write on the blackboard, they also concentrate where they are looking and begin to write at eye level. However, the unskilled blackboard writer often has great difficulty in printing several sentences or lines of information in an orderly, balanced and uniform manner.

The writing on the victim's bathroom mirror is simply too neat and organized to be written by someone expected to be distraught and unfamiliar with writing in a standing position against a smooth, unlined surface. Under stress people generally do what they are normally comfortable doing when they aren't under pressure. If Deceased didn't regularly write on a blackboard, or similar surface, it is highly unlikely that she would have been capable of writing the neatly prepared statement on the mirror after being up all night under the stress described by her husband. It is much more likely that the message was prepared in the early morning hours by someone quite comfortable with writing from a standing position and carefully arranging balanced statements on a blackboard or elevated writing surface.

It would be much more reasonable to believe the victim wrote that message if it was on a piece of paper, written in pen or pencil, which may have been available in her purse, bedroom or the bathroom wastepaper basket. If she was the person who normally cleaned that mirror, and she actually wanted her husband to call her later, it is most unlikely that she would risk antagonizing him by leaving a message he would have to spend time cleaning up. If the black bag on the floor in the bathroom photograph was her purse, and it was inventoried, available writing material would have been noted. Her close friends, and particularly coworkers, should also know if the victim carried writing materials in her purse.

Deceased was almost five inches shorter than her husband. If the crime scene investigator in the bathroom photograph is between 5'7" and 5'10", it is reasonable to believe that (name removed), 5'11", prepared the message. If the investigator's height doesn't fall within that four inch range, it is also reasonable to believe than an experienced (removed) would be comfortable, under stress, writing the first line of an extremely well balanced message above eye level.

In the statements I reviewed, Mr. (name removed) never mentions the lighting conditions when he finally found the victim in the bathroom area. The victim's mother, her former husband and Mr. (NAME REMOVED) were able to describe her sleeping habits, but no one said she ever slept with the light on in her bedroom or in the secluded areas she occasionally retreated to over the years. With no abnormal noise or loud music mentioned in the _____ household that morning, there doesn't appear to be a reasonable explanation for the pillow covering the right side of her head. It does appear that an assailant could have used the pillow to muffle the sound of the shot and/or cover her face.

When a person is suddenly attacked and killed by a family member remorse is often displayed, once the attacker calms down, by covering or shrouding the victim's body. In this case it appears that Deceased was the victim of a planned execution. It is expected that the killer checked the wound on the right side of her head and then chose to cover her face, not as a display of remorse, but rather to cover the unpleasant sight while the killer, and perhaps accomplice, spent time staging the scene in the bathroom.

(name removed) could have kept the victim awake for a portion of the early morning hours to insure she would be very tired and sleep even more soundly than she usually did. This would have also allowed time for (name withheld) to drive to the _____'s home. His statement that his motive for keeping Deceased awake was to prevent her from committing suicide is illogical. He was not preventing her from going into a drug and alcohol induced coma by keeping her awake. If his statements that she wanted to commit suicide were to be believed, he could have simply let her fall asleep and then watch her. There seems to be no reasonable explanation for (name removed) keeping his wife awake, unless it was part of a plan to exhaust her into becoming an easy victim of a homicide which would then be staged to appear as a suicide.

The resistance (name removed) has displayed through his attorney, by not submitting detailed handwriting samples, may be overcome by subpoenaing his personnel records from the local _____ system. Even as a number of years pass a person's printing style generally remains the same. Employment applications, insurance applications, union records and medical forms are often hand printed. If Det. Berry would consider requesting those type of documents for: Deceased, Ex-wife and (name removed) similarities may be recognized in some of their past writings. Also, as suggested by the document examiner, there are several ways to have Mr (name removed and ex-wife recreate a similar message that I will discuss with you at your convenience.

Finally, if Det. Berry isn't permitted to continue to develop enough evidence for a criminal prosecution, the victim's mother and brother should consider a wrongful death suit. With the abundance of circumstantial evidence against Mr. (name removed), they should be able to win the civil case. If Mr. (name removed) refuses to answer questions under oath he will lose the civil case by default. If he did respond to the questions, all his statements and evidence produced during the civil trial could be used by Det. Berry and his prosecutor in a criminal prosecution. Due to the numerous barriers before Det. Berry in his efforts to pursue this case as a homicide investigation, a civil wrongful death suit preceding a criminal prosecution, of at least Mr. (name removed), may present a win-win situation for the Detective and the victim's family.

Sincerely,

Raymond M. Pierce

Answers to the following questions may add to the list of inconsistencies developed in this case by Detective J.C. Berry.

1. Did the telephone records checks verify all the initial statements of (name removed) and his former wife (name removed)?

2. Was the approximate temperature within the victim's bathroom available shortly after the arrival of the first officers on the scene?

3. From the report dated 12/22/99, was (name removed) ever interviewed in depth?

4. Was (name removed) statement, that Deceased had bankrupted him, ever disproved or verified? Were thorough financial checks conducted for (name removed and ex-wife?

5. Was (name removed) late night doctor's appointment disproved or verified? Was a subpoena considered for the doctor's records to determine if a late night appointment would be out of his ordinary pattern of visits?

6. Was ex-wife confronted with Deceased's friend's statement that ex-wife was lying when she told investigators that the victim discussed suicide with frined anytime over the last three years of her life?

7. Does ex-wife statement that she spoke on the telephone to "Deceased's house" from 10PM to 11PM, 12'15'98, conflict with Friend's statement?

8. Were the hairs or fibers recovered from the victim's left hand identified?

9. Were the two recent oval shaped bruises on the victim's lower left knee and upper left shin explained?

10. Was the victim's insurance company identified and notified to withhold payment to potential suspects?

Below is the report that the mother had to order and pay for from Gary Ashenbaugh.

Gary L. Aschenbach
Maryland State Police (ret.)
Licensed Private Investigator

LAW-TECH
Consultants

December 17, 1999

RE: Death Investigation

There are numerous indicators within the oral/transcribed statements made by (husband) that have been identified through *Forensic Statement Analysis* that support his comments as being either untruthful and/or incomplete. This case relates to the death investigation concerning his wife, (name removed) on December (date removed). To begin the analysis, we make reference to the response given by (husband) concerning his detailed account of the events surrounding Mrs. _____ death to Detective Berry. My, uh, **wife was upset** because we'd been having marital problems. We were talking about separating. She had been talking about committing suicide. I had urged her to contact a friend because I was in Olympia going to **the** doctor and I was talking to her on the phone on the way home and she did have a friend come over. Uh, she was going to, uh, leave the house and go with him but she decided not to and, uh, she, she stayed. We were talking. She was talking about committing suicide and I was, uh, trying to talk her out of it and kept her with me and, uh, we discussed it for quite awhile and I was trying to stay awake and keep her with me and make sure she was safe. I thought if she, you know, get through the **morning**, uh, then I'd get her some help **but**, uh, I fell asleep sometime around 5 o'clock in the morning and, uh, when I, my alarm went off at 6, I got up and, uh, she wasn't in bed with me so I went **back** to **check** on her. I **looked**, came out in the living room and then I went **back** in the **back** closet and she was there and she had committed suicide and I didn't, I didn't know it and I didn't hear it until then.

In statement analysis, particularly those cases involving a suspicious death or other violent crimes, we look for indicators to suggest the type of relationship between the victim and witness/suspect. The repeated use and/or non-use of pronouns oftentimes provide clues as to their close or distant relationship. As an example, we ascertain if the suspect referred to the victim as "my wife" or "the wife". My wife obviously indicates a close relationship as opposed to "the wife". In addition, in a truthful statement that reflects reality, we find a person's normal mannerisms, courtesies, and social introductions follow through in their statements. As such, we expect a person mentioned in a story for the first time to be introduced and identified by not only their name, but by their proper title too, as in "My wife (name removed)" This shows respect, sincerity and most likely a caring relationship.

Notice in Mr. (name removed) first statement (page 1), that he never refers to the victim by her given name of "_____". Instead, he only refers to her as "wife", "she", and "her". This already suggests a problematic relationship. The victim is referred to one time as "My, uh, wife" but notice that it was said only after being separated with "uh". When compared to the other uses of "uh" throughout the statement, we find that they appear in areas of sensitivity and perhaps deception. Even though the proper title is used, the separation by "uh" and the missing name of "____" suggests a bad relationship. This is further supported in subsequent comments where Mr. (name removed) claims to have checked "the" victim's pulse. Notice that in addition to omitting her name, he refers to her neck as "the" neck on two occasions. He also said that he checked for "a pulse" and not "her" or "(name)'s" pulse. When used in this context, the word "a" as in a pulse indicates one of many pulses. Would we not expect a caring, sincere husband would refer to his wife's pulse in amore personal manner?

As mentioned above, the continued use of the "uh" sound produced by Mr. (name removed) and its location throughout the statement most likely suggesting that he is stalling in an attempt to formulate an answer. As opposed to a truthful person who does not find it necessary to "pick and choose" what they are about to say in an effort to conceal sensitive information. In statement analysis we concentrate not only on the areas where the "uh" appears, but also where it is absent to determine a change in language. Does its presence suggest stalling and its absence suggest truthfulness? Notice the below comments that do utilize the "uh" and the information which it surrounds.

1. "My, **uh**, wife was upset ..."
2. "**Uh, she** was going to **uh**, leave the house ..."
3. "...she decided not to and, **uh**, she, she stayed."
4. "...I was, **uh**, trying to talk her out of it..."
5. "...any kept her with me and, **uh**, we discussed it..."
6. "get through the morning, **uh**, then I'd get her some help..."
7. "...but, **uh**, I fell asleep sometime around 5 o'clock..."
8. "...**uh**, when I, my alarm went off at 6..."
9. "I got up and **uh**, she wasn't in bed with me..."

It is common and expected that when asked a question concerning an event that occurred in our past, we naturally remember in reality what in fact transpired. If however, that information is sensitive to us, we hesitate and even stall if necessary to allow us to pick and choose what is "safe" to say in order to survive the interview. Notice that after Mr. (name removed) comments that "...**uh**, she wasn't in bed with me..." that he discontinues the use of "uh". At that point, he would have us believe that he just discovered his wife to have committed suicide. Prior to that, he is struggling with the confusion and details of what happened. Since it is true that the victim is dead at that point and the use of "uh" has ceased, we are left to assume that the prior comments in which the "uh" is present, are then sensitive, and most likely untruthful. Why then does he discontinue using the "uh" stalling technique after she is believed to be dead? It is perhaps due to his belief that his story is no longer subject to contradiction, at least not by the victim? Perhaps now he is feeling safe and comfortable to say whatever he chooses without fear of the truth being exposed.

Contrary to an untruthful statement, a truthful person enjoys the "gift of freedom" to speak at length on any question or issue posed to them. The result is an easy to read, chronologically structured story. An untruthful statement on the other hand is found to be erratic, fragmented, and confusing to the reader. Similar to the answer provided by Mr. (name removed). Not only is it peppered with the "uh" to suggest sensitive information, but it offers confusion as to whether he is on the telephone or in person talking to Mrs.____. Again, this supports an untruthful statement where a person is careful to avoid exposing certain information because it may be sensitive to him and in doing so leaves the reader pondering over what really happened or is happening at a particular time within the story.

In that same paragraph, we note the verbs of communication chosen by Mr. (name removed). We commonly find that the use of words such as "talking", "chatting", "said", "spoke to", etc. are generic in that they do not suggest disagreement or an argument. However, the verb "discussed" in most cases does suggest a problem. Notice the verbs of communication below:

1. "We were **talking**..."
2. "She had been **talking**..."
3. "...I was **talking** to her..."
4. "We were **talking**..."
5. "She was **talking**..."
6. "...trying to **talk** her out of it..."
7. "...we **discussed** it..."

A change in language is a change in reality. In statement analysis we attempt to determine if the change in language is justified by the sequence of events. That is, is there a reason why "talking" is finally changed to "discussed"? If there exists an obvious reason for the change then it is justified. If not, then the interviewer is challenged to learn by the change occurred. In the above verbs of communication, we find that "talking" and "talk" are Mr. (name removed) most favored of verbs of communication. These do not normally suggest aggressive, angry, language. However, the word "discussed" changes the reality of the conversation and is most commonly associated with an unfriendly and sometimes aggressive exchange of dialogue between two or more persons. This may suggest that the prior "talking" took a turn for the worse and perhaps escalated to the more aggressive word of "discussed" and possibly violence. After which, you will notice that no dialogue is ever again mentioned between Mr. and Mrs. _____after the verb "discussed" is used. Are we to believe that they had nothing left to say, or perhaps, Mrs. (name removed) met with her demise after the "discussion" took place?

This is further supported where we find the phrase "quite a while". This has been identified along with other phrases and words such as "shortly thereafter", "afterwards", "the next thing I remember", "all of a sudden", etc. to suggest missing time and most often, missing information. This is true particularly when the word or phrase comes at the time of the suspected crime. Mr. (name removed) conveniently placed "quite a while" after there was a discussion. Most likely there is unaccounted for time at that point that requires further investigation. It's important to remember that contrary to popular belief, most people do not lie. Instead, they choose to omit information. By doing so we feel more comfortable with ourselves in that if we get discovered our excuse will not be that I lied, only that I left out information.

Though they "discussed it for quite a while", Mr. (name removed) would now have us believe that he could not stay awake to, as he said, keep her with him and make sure she was safe. In reality, he succeeded in both by having her stay with him and in being safe. Notice that he did not say: "keep us together", which would have been more appropriate to show a close relationship. By separating "her" and "him" with the word "with" actually shows distance, not closeness. Still he kept her with him by not allowing her to leave that morning. Instead, she died as his wife, Mrs. _____. He also stated the he wanted to keep her safe. This too I believe was accomplished in that a person can still be safe (their body) even though they are dead.

This comment came even after his wife allegedly spoke of "committing suicide" on two prior occasions. We are then left to believe that although Mr. (name removed) tried to stay awake to keep his wife safe he ultimately failed to do so. Fortunately, he did remember to set his alarm prior to accidentally falling asleep so that he would be awakened at 6:00, or so he would have us to believe. If he was so concerned for her safety would we not expect that he would have called for professional assistance regardless of the hour of the night or morning? Particularly after her alleged repeated comments of suicide and the missing handgun. Notice that the comment "then I'd get her some help" is also prefaced with "uh" to suggest doubt and possibly deception at that point as well. Given the evidence in this case, it is doubtful that Mr. (name removed) had any intentions of providing the victim with help in any manner.

Mr. (name removed) said that he was awakened at 6 by his alarm clock. Notice that he fell asleep at "5 o'clock" but when his alarm went off, it was a "6". The obvious change is that the "6" is absent "o'clock". Again, a change in language at this point supports deception. Coincidentally, it comes at a point where Mr. (name removed) said: "uh, she wasn't in bed with me".

Jerry C. Berry | WHERE MURDERERS WALK FREE

According to the reporting officers on the scene that morning, only the side of the bed used by Mr. (name removed) appeared slept in. The opposite side where Mrs. _____sleeps was hardly disturbed. Whey[sic] then would he expect her to be asleep in bed with him if she had never been there prior?

Perhaps one of the more significant, contradictory, and most damaging parts of Mr. (name removed)' statement to this point is where he talks of what he did upon awakening. After allegedly noticing that Mrs. _____ was not in bed with him, he commented:

1. "...so I went back to check on her..."
2. "...I looked, came out in the living room..."
3. "and then went back in the back closet..."

In quote number one above, Mr. _____ admitted that he went back to check on her. If he was surprised to learn that she was not in bed with him when he awakened, that clearly indicates that he would not know where she was. Yet his next comment is that he went back to check on her. Two obvious questions need to be asked here: first, how would he have known where to check on her? And second, how can a person go back to do something unless they have already been there on a prior occasion? This clearly suggests that he did know where Mrs. _____ was and that he had obviously been there before. We next have to ask what it was that he was to "check" on? Was it to make certain that she was there, or to make certain that she was dead prior to his calling 911?

In quotes number two and three above, he obviously admitted to looking at her on the floor and then after going in the living room (notice it was not to look for her), and then he returns back to the closet again. We have a tendency sometimes to overlook the obvious and assume what the person meant to say as opposed to what was actually said. In this case, it is obvious that Mr. _____ would have us believe that he went to the living room first and later found Mr. _____ in the back closet. According to his own words, that is not in fact what happened. He is relating to us what transpired in reality from his memory to which he should be held accountable.

As a final thought in that same passage spoken by Mr. _____, he claims that he found Mrs. _____ had committed suicide of which he was not aware of until then. However, his last comment is that he did not "hear" it until then. Is he suggesting that he heard it as he found her on the floor?

Or perhaps, he once again is recalling from his own memory when in fact he did hear the gunshot?

There is a question presented to Mr. _____ concerning the missing gun. Mr. _____ prefaces his comment with the infamous "uh", which already suggests sensitivity and perhaps deception in his answer. In fact you will find that there are three (3) more "uh's" in that same response. Even though he said earlier in the statement that the gun belonged to him from his father, he fails to take ownership of it by making reference to it as "the" gun. We oftentimes find a person attempting to distance himself or herself from an object, an event, or even another person by referring to them as "the" instead of "my". Is it that Mr. _____ would choose to distance himself from the gun because of what he done with it?

Additional clues of an uncaring relationship are found where he, Mr. ___ ___, refers to the bathroom shared by him and the victim as "that" bathroom, instead of "our" bathroom. He also said that she (_____) gave the gun to "her" friend, (name removed) and not "our" friend. Most likely that is a truthful statement. If that were the case then, why would Mr. _____ not be more inquisitive about why his property, given to him by his father, was given to "her" friend ? More interesting, why did Mrs. _____ only give friend the gun and not the holster too? Mr. _____ then "assumed" that her friend had the gun and therefore did not see a need to look for it any longer. While it is speculation on my part, it would appear that Mr. ___ ___ is a possessive type person who most likely always wants more. Why then would he have such little concern for his property that was given to "her" friend without knowing the details, and in particular, when it was to be returned?

In Mr. _____ concluding comment he said, "That's about all I know". This phrase is quite common and unique to someone who is withholding information. When asked a "bi-parlor" question concerning did you tell me everything, a truthful person responds with a simple affirmative "yes". A bi-parlor answer to a bi-parlor question is expected. However, when a person is knowingly withholding information they choose the more popular "evasive verbal response" given by Mr. _____ that suggest untruthful and/or incomplete information at that point.

In this analysis we have identified areas to support the following:

1. An uncaring relationship by the suspect.
2. Verbs of communication to support a dispute/argument.

3. Possible time of death.
4. Sensitive information provided by the suspect.
5. Phrases to suggest incomplete/false information.
6. Changes in language unsupported by the sequence of events.
7. Lack of emotions by the suspect.
8. Obvious "Freudian slips" that most likely come from memory.
9. Psychological distancing from the victim and weapon.
10. Lack of commitment in having told everything.

Statement analysis helps to identify areas within a statement that should be explored further with the witness/suspect. Unfortunately, it is my understanding that Mr. _____refuses to speak to you concerning this investigation. Still, there are other leads you might consider to further your efforts. Perhaps you might consider the following:

1. Transcribe and analyze the 911 call reported by Mr. _____.
2. Have the sons' statements analyzed.
3. Perform handwriting comparison from Mr. _____ and the writing on the mirror.
4. Check for latent prints on the lipstick used to write on the mirror.
5. Identify the sperm from the autopsy & contraceptives in the bathroom.
6. Interview other close friends of Mr. and Mrs. _____.
7. Interview "the" doctor Mr. _____ claims to have seen and medical records.
8. Obtain and compare for contradictions a copy of the cell phone bill in which Mr. _____' claims to have spoken to the victim the night prior.
9. Ascertain if any prints are on the ammunition themselves.
10. Continue attempts to re-interview Mr_____.
11. Offer Forensic Hypnosis to Mr_____ and/or sons for total recall.
12. Have crime scene photos, reports & evidence reviewed for second opinion.
13. Check on any and all insurance policies and recent payments.
14. Consult with your local prosecutor to consider a Grand Jury investigation.
15. Consider an asset investigation to determine ownership and beneficiary(s).
16. Who stands to prosper with the victim's death and how would a divorce have changed those results?

In light of the above findings and from my understanding of the case evidence collected to date, there exists considerable doubt as to how the death of Mrs. _____ actually occurred. By many of Mr. _____ own admissions, he tells us that it did not occur as he would have us believe. It is my opinion that this investigation not be closed as a suicide, but instead be actively investigated to bring it to a successful close.

We wish you the best of luck and invite you to call upon us at any time.

Sincerely,

Gary L. Aschenbach - President
Law-Tech Consultants

With three independent reports, from three recognized experts in the field of homicide investigations, wouldn't you think the Sheriff would have taken steps to put the investigation to rest in an appropriate manner? He should have put all his Detectives and their resources to work and to methodically and systematically resolve each questionable issue surrounding the case. But, that would require some admission on his part that the investigation had been less than professional, and his Detective Sergeant was less than proficient. He had spent a great deal of time campaigning and convincing the citizens he was the greatest thing since sliced bread, and he wasn't going to do anything to hurt that image.

I arrived at the office on the morning of May 3, 2001, and was told by my Sergeant that the Chief Deputy had a meeting scheduled for 10:00 am. I was told that it was for all those who had been involved in the investigation. Apparently he was going to go over Vernon Geberth's report. When 10:00 am rolled around, I walked into the Chief's office to find the Detective Sergeant already there. Behind me came the Deputies who were the first to arrive on the scene. Shortly after they came in, the other four who had some involvement arrived. The Deputy Chief, sitting behind his desk handed out copies of Vernon Geberth's report. He told us to read it. After we had time to complete the reading, he asked each one of us if we thought it was suicide or homicide. Of course, the original Detective was quick to say suicide. Myself, the two Deputies, and the two Patrol Sergeants said homicide. The Detective Sergeant said that he was still undecided but, "was leaning toward homicide now". (That was a shocker!) The Chief tried to make a production out of going over each one of Geberth's points, accusing him of being "unprofessional and biased".

The truth was, the report hit too close to home and made the Department look like idiots. It amazed me that the Sheriff and his Administration couldn't accept the idea that they were less than perfect and that they didn't have a professional Detective Division. The greatest amazement to me was the Sheriff never participated in any of these meetings or put forth any effort to be involved. Not one time did he even attempt to discuss the case with me. I believe that a professional Sheriff not only would have been at the crime scene on the morning of December 16, 1998, but would have been involved on a daily basis. Most certainly he would have been involved in these little meetings that the Chief arranged.

When we were done, I handed the copy of Geberth's report back to the Chief. He told me I could keep it, but I made a point of letting him know in front of the others that I didn't want it. I didn't want him accusing me later of giving the report to anyone else, and I believed that he would do just that, if given the opportunity.

The next day, a Sergeant told me to meet with the Detective Sergeant at 1:00 pm to go over a list of questions the mother of the victim had sent to the Sheriff. At 1:00 pm I was at the office and contacted the Detective Sergeant. We went into a room behind closed doors and sat down at the conference table. He showed me a copy of the letter the mother had sent to the Sheriff, listing over 30 questions she had about the investigation.

He read them off one at a time, asking me for the answer to each one. I provided the answers, and when the session was over, I assumed he would send those answers to the victim's mother, at least in some form or another. Instead, he sent her a short and non-committal type letter.

From Performance Evaluation

.......Dep. Berry is the leader of the squad in areas of calls and reports. He also leads the squad in civil services. I have observed a great dedication to the department in respect to his desire to take on extra investigations........and put extra effort into training his

fellow officers.

Sergeant Kenneth Cheeseman

13

Dixie Harkcom Murder

AT 9:00 PM on October 17, 2000, I was called at home by Dispatch. I was told to respond to Aumiller Road to an elderly female who had been found in the ditch. As I headed out, I was contacted by one of the road Sergeants and told that the victim's husband had found her and called 911. I asked if the scene had been secured and was assured that it had. I was told that the Aid Crew had been brought in and confirmed that the victim was in fact dead.

It was raining hard and I worried about the damage it was going to do to the scene. Shoe prints, tire tracks and trace evidence will wash away quickly. Sometimes something as small as a hair or fiber will be the key element in whether a crime is solved or not. I had more concerns as I learned who the Sergeant on scene was and that the Chief Criminal Deputy was also there. These two guys could never resist the urge to satisfy their curiosity by walking into a scene and looking around. "Another crime scene going to crap before I even get there", I thought.

It was about what I expected when I arrived. Local police had driven their car into the scene, the Aid van had been allowed to drive in, and, of course, the Chief and the Sergeant had been in and out of the area where the body was lying. To get to where the body was, there was a steep decline of about twelve feet from the shoulder of the roadway. At the bottom was a small creek and heavy underbrush. The body was lying on its back, eyes starring blankly. The victim was an elderly female, small in stature, with white hair. She was wearing jeans, a sweat shirt and white tennis shoes. I could see that her shoes were exceptionally clean considering the mud around the area. There were stains on her pants that appeared consistent with her having fallen on her the back.

It was raining so hard that I knew there was no way to preserve the scene. At this point, we still did not know the cause of death. I called for the Coroner and while waiting, I was told that the body had been originally found face down. Apparently, the first responder with the Aid Crew had rolled the body onto its back. My concern now was finding the cause of death as soon as possible. We still didn't know what we had for sure.

When the Deputy Coroner arrived, we went through the usual steps in bagging the hands and trying to preserve any possible evidence. At this time, there was nothing visible to indicate how she had died. After we completed photographing and collecting what we could, we then rolled the body back onto its face. We wanted to get an idea of what position it was in when it was first found. As soon as we started looking closely at the back of the head, we could see a small amount of blood at the base of the neck. Further examination showed a small hole in the middle of the back of the head.

I assisted the Deputy Coroner in bagging the body and getting it up the steep bank to the transport vehicle. I went back to the body site and took one more look around before leaving. Searching a crime scene at night is not the preferred method, and would usually be secured until daylight. But with it raining as hard as it was, and the potential for evidence being washed away, I did the best I could under the circumstances. Before leaving, I made sure that a Deputy had been assigned to guard the scene until the following day. I wanted to come back during the day with help and search the area again.

I knew that a Deputy had obtained a statement from the victim's husband, but I wanted to speak with him myself. I wanted to gauge his reactions and responses to certain questions. In these types of cases, the victim's spouse is always the first suspect, and needs to be either the primary focus of the investigation, or eliminated as soon as possible.

When I arrived at the Harkcom residence, I was greeted at the door by the victim's husband. He led me into the kitchen area and I started by offering my condolences. He had the appearance and demeanor of a man still in shock over what had happened. I knew in my own mind and heart within a few minutes that he had nothing to do with the death of his wife. Even though I felt he was innocent, I went through the interview process with questions that clearly made him realize that he was a suspect. Throughout the entire process, Mr. Harkcom was cooperative and showed no physiological signs usually associated with deception. He told me the following: That his wife worked at the market in Vader, and always liked to walk to and from work on nice days. She was always home when he came in from work, but on this evening she wasn't. He said he made a few phone calls to friends and family, but she was not with any of them. He said the market owner had told him she left the store at her usual time and nothing seemed out of the ordinary.

After several unsuccessful attempts to locate her, Mr. Harkcom got a flashlight and went looking for her. He drove to the market and parked his car. From there, he walked the mile long route that Dixie would have taken, searching the ditches and brush alongside the road. When he got to the location where she was found, he was shining the flashlight down the embankment and into the brush. He knew that there was a trail here that led to their house through the woods. Sometimes Dixie liked to walk that trail the short distance to the house, just to be closer to nature. He saw a plastic bag that he recognized as the type from the market, and knew that Dixie often carried a few things home with her. In the bag were her keys, eye glasses, and a few other personal things she usually carried. He collected the bag, knowing that something was wrong, but he was not prepared for what he found. I can only imagine the sickening and devastating feeling that must have come over him when he saw in the illumination of his flashlight, his beloved wife, face down in the brush. He got close enough to her to know that she was dead and went to the closest house where he called 911.

I told him that we didn't know the cause of death, but we would know the following day. After leaving Mr. Harkcom, I went to his neighbor's house where he had made the 911 call. I interviewed the residents and retrieved the plastic bag that Mr. Harkcom had picked up near the site where he had made the gruesome discovery.

After leaving the residence, I made a few notes and prioritized the things that needed to be done the following day. We still didn't know the cause of death and that had to be the first thing established. I then drove home, knowing that I was in for another sleepless night.

The first thing I did when signing in service the following morning was drive straight to the crime scene. It had stopped raining and looked like it was going to be a clear day. When I arrived, I contacted a Deputy who had worked the graveyard shift guarding the crime scene. He told me that other than a few curious citizens stopping by, nothing unusual occurred during his watch.

I spent the next three hours working through the scene, not finding anything that suggested what had happened to Dixie. I stood on the shoulder of the roadway, first staring down at the crime scene, then looking south at the road, the direction from which Dixie had come. There was a bridge about 75 yards South of the crime scene that crossed a stream, and I walked to it, searching the shoulder and brush on both sides of the road. I took photos of every beer can, piece of paper, and anything else that even looked remotely fresh.

I got a call from the Deputy Coroner on my radio advising me that an autopsy had been scheduled for that afternoon. I responded by ordering the body to be taken immediately to Centralia Providence Hospital. I wanted full body X-rays and an examination by the Attending Physician. The sooner we knew the cause of death, the sooner we could concentrate our focus in the right direction. I advised the Deputy Coroner that I would meet her at the hospital, since I knew she would be there before I would.

As I started my drive to the hospital, I went over what we had so far. We had a crime scene that may have had crucial trace evidence washed away by the heavy rain. We had a body that had been inappropriately moved by the first responding aid personnel. My opinion was that we lacked the assistance of a Medical Examiner or competent Coroner and the assistance of professional investigators. At this time I was still struggling with the incompetence of the other investigations and the lack of interest and participation of the Sheriff. To this point, the Sheriff hadn't even bothered to ask me about the investigation, and I had to assume that one of his team had been keeping him posted. I could feel the stress building already, and it was only the beginning of the investigation into the death of Dixie Harkcom.

I arrived at the hospital and was led into a room where I met with the Attending Physician. He had the X-rays posted on the lighted board and was looking them over. He directed my attention to the X-ray of the head and pointed to a small object lodged in the wall of the skull. It appeared to be a fragment of something, and it was the Physician's opinion that it was a small caliber bullet such as a 22 cal or even a 25 cal. A visible path from the entry wound at the back of the head left little doubt that Dixie Harkcom had been shot. The preliminary examination of the body by the Physician resulted in no findings of further injuries. The body was released to be transported back to the morgue, and I headed for the office to brief the Sheriff and his Administration.

After the briefing, I was assigned a Detective to assist me in the investigation. Kurt was a good cop and had just recently been assigned to the Detective Division. He had no formal homicide investigation training that I was aware of and no actual experience, but he was smart and willing to do whatever was asked of him. This was better than what I had been used to in the way of help.

I ordered the Crime Scene Van to the crime scene and the remainder of the day was spent retrieving the various items I had photographed along side the road. Kurt walked through the scene with me as I pointed out and explained the details of where the body had been found. I wanted him to start analyzing the scene, and start creating his own theories as to the possible manner of death. We knew the cause, a gunshot to the head, but we didn't know the manner or circumstances, sometimes called the mechanism of death.

Because of the time spent at the hospital obtaining X-rays, the autopsy had been rescheduled for the following day. The day finally ended and everyone had signed out of service, but I still had one more chore to take care of, notifying Dixie's family that she had been murdered by a gunshot to the back of the head.

On the way to the Harkcom residence, I kept thinking about how I would tell the family that Dixie had been shot in the back of the head. Families have a hard enough time accepting the news that a loved one had died from natural causes; accepting a murder is another matter. I realized there was not going to be an easy way, so I decided on a direct, straight forward approach.

When I arrived, Mr. Harkcom met me at the door and invited me in. The youngest daughter was there, as well as other family members. They were all sitting quietly just starring at me, waiting for me to give them some answers. After a few seconds of uncomfortable silence I told them. "Mrs. Harkcom died from a single gunshot wound to the back of the head." I figured it was best to get it out as quickly and as simply as possible. Everyone in the room gasped and the reaction of the youngest daughter was just short of getting physically sick. She got up, moving in one direction then another, gasping and obviously in shock. Tom dropped his head and was silent. It was all I could do to keep back my own tears as I watched the horror, shock and grief wash over the family. This was without a doubt, the hardest death information I had ever given. I remembered thinking how quickly a family can be devastated and how quickly a life can be taken. Suddenly I felt the enormity of the responsibility associated with a murder investigation. How anyone involved in law enforcement, especially homicide investigators, take these investigations lightly is beyond me. I remember answering that question to my self. To some it is just a job; a steady paycheck one gets whether a case is solved or not.

After answering a few questions, I asked Mr. Harkcom if he owned any 22 caliber weapons. He said that he did; a rifle. I asked him if I could take a look at it and he agreed. When he returned with it, I told him I needed to take it as potential evidence and have it tested. He told me that he understood the need, and had no problem with me keeping it as long as necessary. I gave my condolences to the family and let them know I would keep them up-to-date as the investigation continued.

The next morning at my office, I concentrated on trying to bring things into some sort of order. It was apparent that this was going to be a difficult case and we needed an investigative plan. Other than the family we didn't have a suspect, and this was the one thing that I wanted to establish as quickly as possible. I knew that this was going to take a combined effort of several investigators and a feeling of despair swept over me at that moment.

I personally thought one of the female Detectives was the best of the group, but she was assigned mainly to child sexual assault investigations and had a full case load of her own. She was my office partner, and at the time I considered her a good friend. She was younger than my daughter, so I had a tendency to be protective of her. We worked a few details together and got along well. Even though she was small in statue, she had a fighter's heart and I knew that she would do her best at any given time. I could always depend on her to give her opinions and ideas and I used her as a sounding board often. She was young, smart, and had the desire to be the best she could be, and was always willing to do her part. She was, and probably still is, a good investigator who has a natural talent when it comes to solving crimes. Because of her case load, I knew that she would only be able to assist at a minimum level. Even though she had little experience in death investigations, I would have preferred her over the others to work with me in the Harkcom murder investigation.

Detective Kurt was also new to the Detective Division. I had worked with him when he was a Patrol Deputy and he seemed like he had a good head on his shoulders. He had no experience in murder investigations, but he knew how to analyze situations. He knew how to work through theories and speculations. This helps an investigator come up with plausible explanations for the many unanswered questions that arise during the course of a major investigation. It looked like it was going to have to be the two of us, so I started laying out an investigative plan based on what little we had so far.

We started by creating our flow charts that would be a visual aid in keeping an ongoing log of our progress. The charts would be broken into categories, each one being modified or added to daily, as the investigation continued. There would be one that displayed the chronology of events and one that would display the potential suspects in order ranging from the most likely to least likely. As each one was interviewed and investigated, the names would be marked through or moved to the right to remain for further consideration. There would be a chart that would log and keep track of every witness and citizen interview. This would be analyzed and each statement given would be corroborated for its veracity. Any uncorroborated or suspicious witness statements would result in that name being moved to the right for further investigation. Similar charts were made for evidence and theories, outlining what may have occurred, based on the combined information produced by all the charts.

We had a murder and no viable suspects! Even though Mr. Harkcom would be considered one and placed at the top of the list, I knew in my heart that he had not killed his wife. I made a list of the known family members and decided we would start with them; asking them about Dixie's relationship with her husband, any known financial problems, and any known disputes with any neighbors. These are the usual questions that will often solicit information that can give insight to a person's lifestyle and even their personality.

Kurt and I spent several days interviewing each family member, taking their statements, noting items of interest, and then comparing them at the end of each day. Each one was added to the flow chart and given their respective place of priority. No one could tell us anything that would even remotely suggest Mr. Harkcom may have killed his wife. There were no financial problems, no history of disputes, no death insurance; nothing!

Two of the family members told us that the husband of Dixie's oldest daughter did not get along with her. We were told that Dixie didn't like him and there had been verbal disputes over different issues. They were convinced that he was the most likely suspect. I felt they wanted the perpetrator so badly that they were clinging to the only thing they could come up with. Since they could not think of another person who would do this horrible thing, they grabbed for the only suspect they could come up with. None of them could tell us anything that could be considered a motive, other than some verbal disputes. However, the son-in-law's name was added to the suspect list under Mr. Harkcom's name. So far, the suspect list looked pretty bleak with only those two names. I wanted to interview the oldest daughter and her husband.

Mr. Harkcom gave me the name and phone number of the oldest daughter who resided in the Spokane, Washington area.

The following day I called the eldest daughter. I identified myself and told her why I was calling. She sounded distant and spoke slowly, as is often the case with those suffering from grief. I asked when she and her husband could come to the Sheriff's Office so I could speak with them in person. She told me they would be there any time I wanted them to be. We agreed on the following afternoon. It is about a six hour drive from Spokane to Chehalis and I hated to have them make the trip, but I needed to interview them both as soon as possible. I was trying to eliminate those initial suspects so we could concentrate our efforts elsewhere. However, I didn't rule out the possibility that the son-in law may be the guilty party. It seemed like a big stretch for him to be the murderer, but we had to treat him like any other suspect until we knew otherwise.

The next morning, Kurt and I went over the things we still needed to do. We decided that we would start contacting every residence that was on the route that Dixie walked to and from work, as well as the residences on the main road where the Harkcoms lived. Maybe some one had seen or heard something and hadn't come forward yet. Sometimes a person will see something and not even realize the importance of it until the right question is asked. It might be as simple as seeing a vehicle that has something unique about it that happened to be in the area. It may be as simple as stopping to assist a motorist change a tire. It wouldn't be the first time a murderer was contacted shortly after the crime.

While Kurt worked on bringing his report and notes up-to-date, I busied myself getting my questions in order for the interviews with Dixie's eldest daughter and her husband. I wondered how the daughter would react when I told her that some of her family had named her husband as a person they suspected of killing her mother. At this point, all had been told was that Dixie had been upset with her son-in-law's political views and she blamed him for taking her daughter away from the area.

When the two arrived, I introduced myself and led them back to the conference room. I told them that I needed to find out everything they could tell me about Dixie and her habits. I then told them that I would like to talk to them individually and they both said they had no problem with that. I asked her to follow me to the interview room. When we were seated at the small table, I asked her about her relationship with her mother. She was very open and forthcoming with her answers. She told me that her mother and her husband didn't get along that well. None of their differences were significant enough to convince me her husband would murder over them. I told her that a couple of her family members had named her husband as a suspect; she didn't seem surprised. She said that she had thought this would happen since the family had somewhat split and taken sides over the disputes. She was adamant that her husband would not have, and could not have committed such a crime. She offered her employer's information and told me I could verify that she and her husband had been in Spokane before, during, and after her mother was murdered. She and her husband both worked for a hospital and the references given were Doctors and Nurses who could verify their statements. After a thorough taped statement, I took her back to the conference room and then had her husband follow me to the interview room. When we both sat down, I told him right out that he had been named as a suspect due to known disputes he had with Dixie. I closely watched his eyes and body movements for any telltale signs of deceptive reactions. Nothing! He leaned forward slightly and looked right at me, his feet squarely on the floor. His forearms were on the table and his hands were open, resting on the table. None of these physical positions were indicative of deception, but rather were strong indicators of a person being truthful. He told me that he had his differences with Dixie but had never entertained the idea of hurting her. He told me that he would do anything I wanted or needed him to do to prove his innocence. He volunteered to take a polygraph test and said he would make himself available at any time I requested. I obtained a taped statement from him and told him that I would like for him to take a polygraph test. I told him that I wanted to eliminate him as a suspect as soon as possible and that was one of the ways to do it. He was quick to agree. I went back to the conference room with him and exchanged email addresses with them. I told them that I would keep them apprised of the investigations and let them know they could contact me at any time.

After they left, I went back to my office and started updating my report. I always tried to keep everything current so it made a clearer, chronological report of events. I packaged the cassette tapes with the statements and placed them into the secretary's in-box so she would get them transcribed as soon as possible. Everything had to be kept current in the event one of the prosecutors wanted to review the reports that we had so far. Plus, it was a lot easier to keep the case file current than to work from memory and notes at a later time.

Kurt came in and asked me how the interviews went. I told him, "no way the son-in-law had anything to do with Dixie's murder". At this point, I was sure of two things: one, was that Mr. Harkcom had not killed his wife, and the other was that the son-in-law had not killed her. So, where did that leave us? We had no motive and no suspects. We had a victim who apparently had no known enemies, no financial problems, no marital problems, and no health issues to contend with. There were no hunting seasons open and nothing in the area where the body had been found to suggest any target practicing had been occurring.

The next morning Kurt and I went to the site where the body had been found. I would start contacting the residences on the East side of the road and Kurt would contact those on the West side. We would meet at the little store where Dixie worked in the town of Vader.

I got to the store a little before Kurt and talked to the store owner. Standing at the counter, I could see a picture of Dixie on the wall behind the store owner. There was also a picture of both of Dixie's daughters. This is typical in small communities where everyone knows everyone and close bonds are made. I got the exact time that Dixie had left the store that fateful day and this would be instrumental in developing an approximate time of death. We knew when she left the store and we knew when her husband had found her. That left a specific time frame we had to work with. I still wanted to close the time frame down even more, so when Kurt arrived I decided to walk the distance from the store to the site where Dixie had been found. We had been told by family members that Dixie usually walked at a brisk pace, and that she knew the shortcuts through the woods to her house. We walked the distance the first time at what we thought would be a brisk pace without stopping. It took us 16 minutes. We then went back to the store and walked it again, this time with Kurt on one side of the road and me on the other. We were looking in the ditches along side the road and fence lines hoping to find some evidence. Anything at all would be examined. We found nothing of value as evidence or anything even remotely suspicious.

We spent the next several days contacting neighbors and locals, hoping to find someone who may have some information that would lead to a viable suspect. We went on one goose chase after another as names of known "dirt bags" were given to us. We contacted every one of them - some were asked to take polygraphs. Still, nothing!

Over the next few weeks, I kept in touch with Mr. Harkcom and his eldest daughter. I knew that the youngest daughter and her Aunt were upset with me because I wouldn't keep working on the son-in-law as the primary suspect. Nothing I said or did would convince them that he was innocent. Even though he had passed the polygraph with a very high score, I began to believe they wanted him to be the suspect. They probably became even more upset with me when I stopped returning their calls. I basically got tired of them complaining that we weren't doing enough and that they had a right to know every move we were making. I decided that Mr. Harkcom was the one who had a right to expect to be kept apprised on a regular basis, and I would leave it up to him to talk to the family. The investigation was frustrating enough without having to contend with disgruntled family members. I have often wondered if a victim's family ever considers what the investigators go through. I'm not talking about the typical Lewis County Sheriff's Office Detectives, but investigators who put their very soul and being into their work. Do they think they just go home at night and forget about it? God, if they only knew!

January 13, 2001
To Whom It May Concern,
I am writing this letter as the only means that I am aware of in an attempt to acknowledge the services and dedication of Jerry Berry.

Jerry has been the lead Detective assigned to my mothers homicide case, Dixie Lee Harkcom, on October 17, 2000. Jerry from the beginning has represented the county as a professional as well as an empathetic individual with a goal to solve this case. Jerry has been put in extremely difficult circumstances of questioning my family and was able to manage our grief, while maintaining empathy, in an attempt to obtain information pertinent to the case. Jerry and many other members of the Sheriff's department have been readily available to me at all hours of the day in addressing any questions, concerns and/or just needing to have someone to talk to about the case. The loss of my mother is great however could have been made worse if someone less skilled would have been handling this case.

Jerry has put many hours into my mother's case; I'm sure more than he actually paid for. Having a father-in-law who is a retired homicide Detective has given understanding of the sacrifices that both these individuals and their families must endure in an attempt to bring some form of closure for others that are or have been in my situation. I hope that the sacrifices that Jerry and the others like him have made are never forgotten and continue to be acknowledged by the department, community and families involved. It is my hope that the Sheriff's department acknowledges the skilled and devoted man that they have and do not overlook these qualities because the loss would be to great for everyone. I will never be able to repay Jerry for his kindness and skills of managing this case but do hope that my words of Thankfulness are heard by all.

Jerry you are a good professional but most of all a great person. Thank you for your professional approach and kindness.

*Sincerely,
Leigh Harkcom-Sefton*

After several weeks without any luck or success, we were given a name of a person who lived Longview, Washington. He was reported to have an outstanding warrant out of Lewis County, and had lived in the Vader area at some time in his past. This was not much, but it was better than what we had come up with so far. We decided to have him picked up on the warrant and brought to Lewis County. I made arrangements with the Deputies to hook him up and notify me when they had him at the Jail. The next day the suspect was booked into the Lewis County Jail on the outstanding warrant. I went down and brought him up the interview room. He was about 5'8", 150 lbs, balding, and looked "down and out." He was about 50 years old and had a history of petty crimes, mainly thefts. We had him tell us about his time in Vader, the people he knew, and the usual background probe. Then we asked him if he knew Dixie Harkcom. He stumbled for words and then said it might sound familiar, but he wasn't sure. I thought, "This guy is a flake" and I had the feeling he was hiding something. We then started a more accusatory type interrogation, trying to get him to give up whatever he was holding from us. After about two hours, we decided to give him a break from the pressure we had placed on him. He agreed to take a polygraph and I told him I would arrange for it the next day.

I called the local polygraph technician and he agreed to conduct the test for us on the following day. If all went well, the guy would either pass with high marks, or would fail and then confess. Continuing the investigation, and the manner in which we would proceed, all hinged on the results of the polygraph test.

The following day we met with and briefed the polygraph examiner, giving him the basic information and the relative questions we wanted him to concentrate on. The questions we wanted him to ask the suspect were simple and straightforward and required only a yes or no; nothing confusing or tricky. The questions were: Did you shoot Dixie Harkcom? Do you have any information about the death of Dixie Harkcom that you have not told law enforcement? Do you know who shot Dixie Harkcom? The test would be run three times with the order of the questions being changed each time. The suspect would be told in advance how the test would be administered so he would not be subjected to any surprises.

We brought our suspect up from the Jail and introduced him to the

Polygraph Examiner. We left them alone and decided to have lunch while we were waiting for the results. The test would take about two hours and there was nothing to do but wait. During the two hour wait, we discussed what we would do in the event the suspect passed the polygraph. This would basically put us back to where we were, no suspects and no clear direction as to how to proceed. If the suspect failed, then I would have to go straight into post-polygraph interview/interrogation techniques as soon after the test as possible. Immediately after a polygraph, the suspect will usually be the most vulnerable and more susceptible to the right interviewing techniques. Generally speaking, when a suspect fails a polygraph, they tend to become scared and confused. Scared because they believe law enforcement now knows the truth, plus the test has a huge physiological impact, confused because they are forced to think as fast as they can, trying to answer the steady barrage of questions by the interrogators while at the same time, trying to decide whether to confess or keep lying. This is a critical time for the investigators. The right theme has to be developed and the right demeanor displayed at the right time. The theme can be developed early on in the interview process. It may be religion, hunting, fishing, or anything that the suspect can relate to. Then a connection is made between the interviewer and the suspect, that is, something in common. It is human nature to be more at ease when talking to others about something that both parties know about and share a common interest in. A great deal of time can be spent in this phase of the interview and should never be rushed. This is where the trust building phase begins. When the suspect believes that the interviewer is being honest and sincere, then a confession is much more likely.

I was waiting anxiously in my office when the Polygraph Examiner came in. He said, "Well, the results show he was deceptive in all his answers, I am going to have to give him a fail". It was hard to hide the excitement that was building within me. "Does he know he failed" I asked. "No, I thought I would let you decide the next move" he replied. I called Kurt in and gave him the news. I could see that he was as excited as I was. Kurt, the examiner, and I went back into the room and I let the examiner explain the results. The suspect didn't say anything, just looked at us. I would have been having a fit if it were me. After the examiner left the room, I started the interview, telling him how sorry I was that he had not passed the lie detector test. I always used the term "lie detector" when talking to a suspect. It was just another little physiological ploy and seemed to have a greater impact on the suspect.

No matter what I tried, I could not find a theme with this guy. The "good guy" approach was not working. After about two hours of soft interviewing, I proceeded to the hard line accusatory interrogation. It came down to keeping at it until he broke and gave us the truth or invoked his rights. The suspect kept up his denial and kept telling us he had not killed anyone and he didn't know why he had failed the lie detector test. The more he denied it, the more we told him that we knew he did it, but he never changed his story. After another two hours, we finally realized that we were not going to get a confession and we took him back to the Jail. We did get names of a few family members and friends of his that were in the Longview area, but that was all we got. By now it was late in the evening so we updated our reports and went home.

The next morning, I briefed my Detective Sergeant and got his approval for Kurt and I to drive to Longview. I told him that we may be late getting back due to the number of people we were going to try and interview, which were the friends and family of the suspect. He showed his usual amount of interest and reminded me to "watch the overtime".

Kurt and I arrived in Longview about Noon and stopped by the Longview Police Department to let the Chief know that we were in their city on official business and briefed the Detective Sergeant. We then drove across town to an apartment complex where the suspect's girlfriend was supposed to live. We were lucky in that she was home and willing to talk to us. We were invited in and I explained to her that her boyfriend had been arrested on a Lewis County warrant. I didn't tell her about him being a suspect in a murder at first. We talked for about 30 minutes, getting some basic background information about her relationship with the suspect and what she knew about his past. She didn't have a lot of useful information and seemed to know very little about his past. When I told her that he was a suspect in a murder, she seemed genuinely stunned at the news. She said he had been working for a local painter during the time of the murder and gave us the name of the contractor. She didn't believe that he was capable of killing anyone and said she would do whatever she could to help us. We left her apartment and then contacted the painting contractor next. The contractor verified that the suspect did work for him. When we insisted that he check his records for the specific day that Dixie was shot, it turned out that our suspect had not worked that particular day!

We made a few more stops that had negative results. When we arrived at the suspect's sister's house, it was about 8:00pm and dark outside. This was the place where he had been living when he was arrested on the warrant. We were greeted at the door by a male who identified himself as the suspect's brother-in-law. When I identified myself and told him we needed to talk about his brother-in-law, we were invited in. We were introduced to a female who was the suspect's sister. I started by confirming that the suspect did in fact live there. Then I asked if they knew if he owned a 22 caliber rifle or handgun. We were told that he did own a 22 rifle and that he had recently put it between the mattresses in his bedroom. It took everything Kurt and I had to remain calm! This had to be the beginning of the end for our suspect! I asked to see the rifle and avoided answering their questions about why we were interested in the rifle. When the rifle was brought out and handed to me, I then told them that we were seizing the weapon as evidence. I wanted to make sure I had my hands on it before I let them know that we were going to be taking it with us. I then told them about the murder, the suspect missing work the day of the murder, his failing a polygraph, and that a 22 caliber weapon had been used to commit the crime. They were shocked to say the least, but surprisingly understanding in what we were doing. We provided them with the usual receipt for the weapon and obtained statements from them.

When we got back into the car and pulled out of the drive way, we both let out our excitement! We knew we had our killer, and we knew we had the murder weapon. The trip back to Lewis County was a lot quicker and more joyous than the trip to Longview had been. On the way home, we talked about how we would proceed the following day. We could go home and get a decent night's rest, a first in many days.

We stopped at the Lewis County Sheriff's Office around midnight and logged the rifle into the Evidence Room. I had another 40 minute drive East to my residence and Kurt had about the same drive time West.

The next day, I was up early and at the office before any of the others arrived. I had gotten a good night's sleep and it felt good to feel somewhat rested. When the Detective Sergeant arrived, Kurt and I briefed him and then we briefed the administration. Everyone felt some relief in the knowledge that we may have Dixie Harkcom's murderer in custody. Before any referrals to the Prosecutor's Office were made, we had a few things to take care of in order to present a solid case. I contacted the Evidence Clerk and requested the rifle be taken to the Crime Lab in Tacoma, along with the bullet that had been recovered from the victim. I wanted a ballistics test conducted as soon as possible. Matching the bullet to the rifle would seal our case and the suspect would be charged as soon as I got the word from the Lab.

After the rifle was on its way, I called downstairs to the Jail and asked that the suspect be brought up to my office. We were sure we had all we needed now to make an arrest, with or without a confession. I wanted to see the suspect squirm when we told him we had the weapon he used, that we knew he had missed work that particular day. And, I knew that an offer of a lesser charge, if he cooperated, might prompt him to give up any accomplices that he may have had.

When he sat down at the table across from us, I told him that we recovered the murder weapon and filled him in on everything we had found in Longview. I told him that the gun was being tested as we spoke and that he needed to help himself. He became very frustrated and started the same pattern of denials as the previous interview. He kept repeating that he had not shot Dixie and that the gun we recovered had not been used in any shootings. It was a repeat of the first interview! He never changed his story or faltered in his denials. I told him that when the ballistic tests were completed and if they matched with the bullet taken from the victim, that he would be charged and I wouldn't be back to give him another chance. His only response was, "It doesn't matter, I didn't shoot anyone".

The following day, I got a call from the Crime Lab in Tacoma. The 22 caliber rifle that I had sent to them had been test fired and the ballistics test were completed. The results showed that the bullet from the gun had a different grove pattern and the "twists" were the opposite from the bullet that had been removed from the victim. The rifle was not the murder weapon. I listened in silence as the Lab Technician completed his verbal report. I barely remember the rest of the conversation, as the feeling of despair swept over me. We seemed so close, with our suspect failing the polygraph, his missing work the day of the shooting, and having found the same caliber weapon at his residence. I thought about one of the other cases with no justice. "God, don't let me have another killing with the murderers walking free!"

I broke the news to Detective Wetzold and the others. We were back to square one and no suspects! I started the arduous process of reviewing the case file, photographs, evidence we had collected and the investigative flow charts. It seemed like I had reviewed these a hundred times hoping to find something we had missed. In my mind I kept seeing the elderly victim, lying dead in the cold rain and wet brush. A vision of her trying desperately to escape her assailants by heading into the brushy wooded area was vivid as I tried to imagine the fear she must have felt. At one point, when she jumped across the small creek and started up the brushy bank into the trees, she must have thought that she had a chance. Familiarity with the wooded area and how to get to the safety of her home through them must have brought some degree of comfort to her for a brief moment. Then a shot rang out, and her life was taken that quick. And she had done nothing to anyone.

A few more weeks went by and nothing had turned up to help in the investigation.

We couldn't think of anything else we could do, or anyone else to talk to. We used the local press, encouraging anyone with information to contact us, yet not a single call or response of any kind!

It was about 9:00 am one morning and I was sitting at my desk when a Deputy came in. He asked how the Harkcom case was coming. I knew he had an interest in investigations and he had spent the first night guarding the crime scene, so I brought him up-to-date. Then he asked me if I had talked to one of the other Detective's friend that had been parked on the roadway close to the time and location of Dixie's murder. I asked him what he was talking about. He said, "Oh, I thought he would have told you." He went on to say that the Detective had told him that he knew a guy who had been parked on the road near the place and time it occurred. He told me that the guy was a friend of the Detective and that he worked for the Railroad. The look on my face must have told the Deputy that I was really getting upset, because I had not heard of any of this. He told me that he just assumed that I knew and said," I can't believe that he didn't tell you that the guy had spoke to Dixie when she walked by him". I thanked him and told him I would talk to the Detective. After the Deputy left I looked at Kurt, he was looking at me, and we both said at the same time, "Can you believe that?" There is no way to adequately described how I felt at that moment. I remember thinking "was there no end to the stupidity, and lack of professionalism?" The Deputy must have stopped by the other Detective's office on his way out, because it wasn't long until he walked in.

I looked at him and asked, "Just when exactly were you going to tell us about the guy that had been in the area when Dixie was murdered?" His reply, "Uh---I guess whenever I thought it might be important". He knew I was mad and I didn't care. I fired back at him, "The man is a potential witness, for God's sake! And you don't think it is important?" He stumbled for words and gave the half-excuse that his friend, who was married, "had been meeting with another woman" and he and "promised that he wouldn't say anything." He went on to tell us that his friend was having an affair and didn't want the wife to know. I knew my voice was getting louder as I practically yelled, "We're not babysitters; it's not your place to help him keep his affair away from his wife!" His only defense was, " but I promised him I wouldn't say anything." If the guy had spoken to Dixie when she walked by, then we knew that he had been there within minutes of when the shooting occurred, and he may have seen the suspects and their vehicle. I was so mad I could hardly keep myself in check. The investigation was weeks old, and one of our own Detectives had been withholding information about potential witnesses, his friend and his friend's "other woman." I told him that he had been withholding evidence in a murder, and the best he could come up with was, "but I promised him I wouldn't say anything, and my word is important to me." I had to leave it at that. How do you respond to that kind of logic?

By this time I had become so disgusted with the Sheriff that I had developed an ulcer, and it was acting up big time! Still dealing with the Sheriff and his Administration over the other death investigations, combined with Detective stupidity was taking its toll on me. My patience was wearing thin as I headed for the Sergeant's office.

I contacted the Sergeant and told him about the potential witnesses that had been kept from us. He was pretty much non-committal and told me to locate and interview them. I was hoping for a little more concern from my Sergeant regarding the withholding of information, but it wasn't going to happen. I then told him that I wanted to go see the Prosecutor about charges of Obstructing Justice and Withholding Evidence. The Sergeant's face turned dark red and said, "We're not seeing the Prosecutor and we're not charging anyone." I just turned and walked out of his office even more disgusted.

Detective Wetzold and I spent the next few days making contact with the Detective's friend and obtained a statement. We then contacted the woman and obtained a statement from her. Apparently, the Detective's friend had met with the woman the day of the shooting as pre-arranged. They had met in a wide gravel area alongside the road about three hundred yards from where Dixie had been shot. They were both in the Railroad Company's pickup truck when Dixie walked by on her way home. She had recognized the guy and said hello to him as she went by. It seems that the guy and woman left very soon after; driving in the same direction that Dixie had been walking. It turned out that the guy had driven past Dixie within minutes after she had fallen to the ground from a gunshot to the back of the head.

At the time, we considered the guy as a viable suspect. He had admitted to being in the area at or near the time of the shooting. He had admitted to seeing Dixie on the road. He admitted to being with another woman, and that could be considered a motive for getting rid of a witness who saw them together.

The days went on, and then one morning I got a call from a Detective with the Cowlitz County Sheriff's Office. He told me they had arrested three "dopers" and they were currently in Jail. One of those arrested had made a comment to another inmate about "an old lady" that had been shot in Lewis County. The inmate that had been given the information then contacted the Detective with the information. The Detective having read our previous teletypes called the Lewis County Sheriff's Office, then being directed to me. After getting what little the Detective had, I called Kurt into my office. I instructed him to drive to Longview and contact the Detective I had just spoken with. I told him to take the female Detective with him, in case there were any female suspects that may need to be interviewed. I wanted them to make a preliminary assessment of the three "dopers" Cowlitz County had arrested, and determine if there were any connections to the Harkcom murder. If there was any validity to the information, I would contact the suspects and conduct the interrogation.

It was during this time frame that I had been told I was going to be put back on the road as a Patrol Deputy, having completed my rotational period. I had been lucky enough to stay in the Detective Division for five years, which was three years longer than the vast majority of my predecessors. It was because of the quality of my work and the high ratio of solved cases that I had been granted yearly extensions after the basic two year period was up. At least that was the reasons I had been given by the Sheriff and his Administration. It was about this time that one of the Sergeants had been promoted to "Inspector", which I believed was the Sheriff's way of having a Lieutenant that he thought he could control. The real Lieutenant had been removed from the position (unofficially of course) and given another job description that kept him out of the mainstream of law enforcement. He too, had made the unforgivable mistake of standing up to the tyrannical dictatorship of the Sheriff and his Administration. The Sergeant or "Inspector" had talked the Chief Deputy into letting me stay another year in the Detective Division a few days before the call from the Cowlitz County Detective came in. I was grateful for that, short lived as it turned out to be.

I had sent the two Detectives to Longview and they departed around 9:00 a.m. that morning. I had been in hot water with the Administration ever since I refused to accept one of the other death investigation as a suicide, and they had pretty much taken all my motivation away. I was depressed, sick of the "hillbilly mentality" of the Sheriff's Office in general, and was drawing further away from the pride I once had in being a Lewis County Sheriff's employee. I was sitting at my desk at around 10:00 am when the Inspector and the Chief came to the door. The Chief told me that they had just received a call from the Forest Service. They had a man in custody who had confessed to them that he had shot another camper near Mt Rainier. The Forest Service had been to the scene and confirmed that a man had been shot and was in fact deceased. The Chief said he was calling the Detectives back from Longview and have them respond to the Mt. Rainier area to "investigate". Now for the reader, keep in mind that the two Detectives were in Longview, Washington at this time. Longview is about 40 miles south of Chehalis on Interstate 5. Mt Rainier is about 70 miles North by Northwest of Chehalis. That put the other two Detectives over one hundred miles from the scene.

Neither one of them were experienced homicide investigators and neither one of them had the sophisticated interviewing/interrogation training that I had. I reminded the Inspector and the Chief Deputy that the other Detectives were in Longview on an assignment regarding the Dixie Harkcom murder. I suggested that I could go to the Mt. Rainier location since I was much closer. I suggested that since I was the more experienced, I could make a quicker assessment of the crime scene and obtain the confession from the suspect. Since he had apparently already confessed to the Forest Service enforcement personnel, the rest should be easy. My thoughts were the other two Detectives could finish their assignment which was also a murder investigation and I could perform a much quicker and more thorough investigation and everyone would win. It seemed like the most logical and sensible way to me. However, I forgot who I was dealing with! The Chief Deputy wouldn't even consider it and his response was, "They need the experience and they are going to do it." I had almost had resurgence of interest and loyalty, and for what?

The two Detectives arrived back at the office a couple of hours later. The female Detective was visibly upset. She told me that she didn't understand why she had been called all the way back to the office when I could have taken care of the Mt. Rainier case. She said that she liked to assist in homicide investigations, "but did not want to be a lead in one." She readily admitted that she didn't have the experience or training to be comfortable in being the lead on a murder case. Kurt was pretty much non-committal and didn't say much one way or the other. I told them both I had tried to talk the Chief and Inspector into letting me handle it since I was so much closer, but had been unsuccessful. I then told them the Cheif had already sent the Crime Scene Van to the scene with the Evidence Clerk, who was also a non-experienced homicide investigator. I knew since that so much time had gone by, and with the Chief being involved, they could rest assured that the crime scene would be contaminated when they got there.

By now it was about time for me to head home, but before I did, the Inspector came to me and told me that the Chief had changed his mind. I was told that I would be going back on the road as a Patrol Deputy after all. It was another way to screw over me for objecting to what I considered to be their idiotic logic in handling the Mt Rainier shooting. So, now we had unfinished business in Longview that would be put off, I was going back on the road, three shootings that needed to be solved; the so called suicide death, the Harkcom death, and the Mt. Rainier shooting.

The following morning when I arrived at the office, I begin the process of cleaning out my office and tying up loose ends on some of the cases I had been working. The Detective Sergeant would have to reassign some of them, the others I closed, if warranted. I told the Inspector that the person of interest in the Cowlitz County Jail still needed to be contacted and told him the Detective Sergeant had given all the information to Kurt. They had decided that Kurt would take over the Harkcom homicide investigation and that he and the female Detecive would work the Mt. Rainier shooting together. Seemed rather stupid to me to take an experienced homicide investigator off of a case that had the potential of being cleared with arrests, at a time when experience and training would count the most.

It is not my intentions to come across as an "expert" because I'm not. I made my share of mistakes, but I learned from them, and the fact remains I had more experience and training than the others. I also had a higher clearance rate than the others. So at a time a murder investigation was at the most critical juncture, I believe a reasonable, rational thinking person would have concluded it prudent to let the lead investigator finish the job he had started.

As I began my duties back on the road, I could not keep from thinking about the shootings that still needed a conclusion. I contacted Kurt after about three days, only to find that they had not charged the suspect in the Mt Rainier shooting. Kurt had not been successful in his interview with the suspect who had supposedly already confessed to the Forest Service law enforcement. From reading his reports, they had not spent that much time at the murder scene and had missed several key elements in interviewing the suspect. Too much time had been wasted in traveling from Longview to the Courthouse, on briefing and preparations, and traveling to Mt Rainier. The critical period for successful suspect interviewing had long since lapsed and the suspect had regained some composure by the time they got to him. Without going into further details, it would be years later before the suspect would be charged with a crime. But another murderer walked free unnecessarily for a very long time.

On March 2, 2004, I received a message from a source at the Lewis County Sheriff's Office. The message was the Chief Deputy had been on the radio praising the Sheriff's Office for solving the Mt. Rainer shooting. It is always good news to hear about a murder being solved, even though this one could have and should have been solved the day it occurred three years ago. But, this would be so typical of the Sheriff and his team, to try to capitalize on the arrest and let the citizens believe it was a great accomplishment. If it had not been for the stupidity of the Chief Criminal Deputy three years ago, the killer would already be serving his time. New deputies reviewed the three year old case and did what could have been easily done when it occurred. However, they are to be commended, for they were not part of the original fiasco.

Supervisors "For All You Do Award"

Detective Berry received this award for a number of reasons, including the amount of work he put into developing and coordinating the Defensive Tactics Program, for his work on the Tripp forgery case where Jerry assisted patrol, and several other cases in the Onalaska area. He also responded to several calls, when patrol was backed up and worked with Deputy Davidson on clearing a number of burglaries and car prowls in the Onalaska area. Detective Berry additionally adjusted his shift so that he could attend an 11 week homicide course in Bellevue. This was very practical training and it takes a big effort on the part of the officer who wishes to attend this, due to the distance and the scheduling times. As we all know, Jerry is willing to help out wherever the need is necessary.
Sergeant Glade Austin , on behalf of the Lieutenant and all the Sergeants

14

JOHN MCCROSKEY WAS a Sergeant and the K9 officer when I went to work for the Sheriff's Office in 1991. I never worked with him and knew him by sight, name, and reputation only. I didn't pay too much attention to his reputation because I always form my own opinions based on my personal contact with any individual. There are always those who are jealous and resentful of authority and positions of power, so I credited the rumors and his reputation to those. An occasional hello in the hallway was the extent of our contacts.

He was assigned to the "Special Services" unit which consisted of Boat Patrol, D.A.R.E., and any public functions. This gave him plenty of public exposure and the opportunity to campaign on-duty. He took advantage of it and whether it is right or wrong, it was a political advantage which paid off for him. He knew how to play the political game and he knew what he wanted out of it.

When it became apparent that Sheriff Bill Logan was going to retire in 1995, there were several men making their plans to run for the position. I was one of them. I had not planned on running for Sheriff this early in my career, but with the incumbent going out, I figured it was a good time to try it. I was the only candidate who ran as an Independent. McCroskey ran on the Republican ticket, as did Norm Wold ,"Mac" McPherson and Bob Nix. On the Democratic side there were Dick Withrow and Grover Laseke. Norm was a Sergeant with the Lewis County Sheriff's Office, as was Dick. Grover was the Chief Civil Deputy with the Department and I was a Deputy. Mac was the Chief of the Town of Winlock located in Central Lewis County.

Without going into great detail about the election year, I was the only candidate that came out of the election still on speaking terms with McCroskey. I ran a clean campaign and he appreciated it. At least I thought he did. Had I known what the others knew at the time, I would have joined them before the general election to smear him out of the race. But I still believed that honesty was better than mud slinging. As a result of me not publicly siding with them, they never came out with McCrosky's skeletons as they planned.

After the election was over and it was official that McCroskey would be our new Sheriff, I went to him and offered my support. I still believed that the open honest campaign I ran would eventually pay off for me. I then spent the next four years busting my butt trying to show him my abilities and worth to his administration. I had the highest clearances in crimes investigated and was the only person to date to fill up both evidence storage areas at the same time with recovered stolen property. I started and maintained a Sheriff's Honor Guard and set up the first fully certified Defensive Tactics Program. I was asked to be the Treasurer for the Awards Committee. I volunteered time to speak at Senior Citizen Centers, teaching home safety and self-protection classes. As time went on, I saw McCroskey make appointments to his administration and I was always a little disappointed that he had passed me over. Then when it came time for a new Sergeant's position, I studied hard for several weeks preparing for the assessment center. I felt good going into the test and knew when it was over that I had done OK. The Sheriff was hot to get the new position filled and had been pushing hard for it.

After about two weeks of waiting for the results, they were finally in. I was called into his office and told, "I've got good news and I've got bad news." I had no idea where this was going so I waited for him to finish. He finished with this, "the good news is that you finished number one in the Sergeant's exam, the bad news is that the Commissioners pulled the funds for the position." I was stunned! No matter how hard I worked, no matter how many hours I put in without pay, no matter how hard I tried, it had just become obvious that I was not going to ever be a part of his Administration.

I have my doubts about whether or not the funds were actually pulled. I rather think had I not finished so high in the exams that he would have filled the position with someone other than me.

I continued to give my best and went through the process of applying and interviewing for each position that became available. Each time, I was passed over. I knew I had been better prepared than the other applicants, and yet I knew each time I would be passed over. I finally came to terms with the fact that I was never going to be promoted under McCroskey's Administration. If they had a specific reason or it was something personal, then I wished they would have just told me. Considering the people McCroskey chose, I am glad now that I never became "one of them".

Letter to Sheriff McCroskey from Hillsboro, Oregon Police Department.
Dear Sir:

This is a letter of thanks for the assistance this agency received from Detective Jerry Berry for a case of in home sexual abuse. Detective Berry interviewed the suspect who was in custody of the Lewis County Jail and obtained a taped confession. Detective Berry was contacted on February 26, 1999 and was supplied with only limited amounts of information concerning the case. Detective Berry was able to use that information to obtain a confession.

Detective Berry should be commended for his attention to duty, interviewing skills, and generally going above the call of duty to assist our agency. Detective Berry's interview supplied the case agent with enough information to obtain an arrest warrant for the suspect.

The victim's family is receiving some level of comfort in this terrible incident thanks to the confession obtained by Detective Berry.

Detective Berry has shown this agency a great deal of professional courtesy and hopefully we will be able to return the favor.

Sincerely,

Detective Theodore Schrader
Chief Ron Lewis

15

Nearing the End

THINGS WERE NOT the same on the road as they were when I was working the East end of the County five years before. The Sheriff's policy of making everyone feel warm and fuzzy had taken precedence over catching the bad guy. It seemed as if greater emphasis had been placed on quick responses to barking dog complaints and less on crime and the drug war. Meth labs and dealings were at an all time high, and nothing was being done about it, as far as I could tell. It seemed as if I couldn't do anything right, being called in at unexpected times for what the Sheriff's Administration referred to as a "consultation." The pressure was mounting and I knew that I had to get out. Staying in a hostile work environment would only lead to more trouble for everyone.

The very site of the Sheriff and the Chief Criminal Deputy made me sick! I had never before experienced so much contempt for another human being, and I knew it was time to get away from them. A few days later I quit.

Even after I left, I tried to keep apprised of how the Harkcom murder investigation was going. You can't spend that much time with a victim's family, and everything else that comes with a murder, to not feel a personal attachment. I still had friends in the Sheriff's Office who kept me updated, as well as the local newspaper. Just towards the end of the Harkcom murder investigation, four suspects were located and confirmation had been made as to their involvement. The information turned up the following scenario:

The four men had driven to Vader from Longview. They had been parked on Aumiller Road when Dixie walked up on them on her way home. She surprised them and witnessed them "shooting up" dope. Apparently they were already well under the influence and panicked. Words were exchanged and Dixie took off running down over the bank. As she crossed the small creek and started up through the brush, one of the suspects fired a single shot from a pistol, striking her in the back of the head. They immediately took off, heading West, then turning South on Highway 603, a few hundreds away. It must have been only minutes until the Detective's friend drove by, just short of seeing the fleeing suspects. Dixie was lying just off the roadway, already dead or in the process of dying at the time.

As I watched the News and read the papers, there was apparently a problem developing in the case. Apparently there had been some serious mistakes made by the Detectives and the Prosecutor was only going to charge one person with a crime. I had the opportunity to speak with the Prosecutor before the Harkcom murder trial and he was displeased with the way the investigation had turned out. He made the comment to me, "if you had finished the investigation, I would probably be charging four instead of one." Even though I know he didn't care much for my outgoing, say-what-I-think personality, I took it as a compliment.

The sad part about this whole investigation, is that the problems and issues resulted in three of the four original murder suspects walking away free. It is my opinion that this can be directly attributed to the Sheriff's Chief Criminal Deptuy, and the Sheriff himself; the Chief Deputy because his vindictiveness and desire to punish me was greater than his ability or desire to see a case solved, and the Sheriff because of his lack of leadership ability, concern, or interest in his Investigative Unit.

16

Frustrations Catch Up

THE FRUSTRATIONS AND pent-up anger finally got the best of me one day while attempting to return a pair of uniform pants. I had ordered the pants from the usual dealer in Tacoma. When they arrived, I did what I have always done with new clothes, and that is remove all the tags before trying them on. After all, the size was correct and what I had ordered. I put them in the closet and several weeks later pulled them out to get dressed for work. When I put them on, they were so small around the waist I couldn't pull them together enough to hook the snap. I had gained a lot more weight than I realized since the last time I had been on the road as a Patrol Deputy. My wife Susan and I were going to Seattle the next day so I decided to take them by the store rather than send them via the Postal Service. When we arrived at the uniform shop, I told the clerk that the pants were too small; emphasizing that it was my fault and not theirs. They had, after all, sent the size I ordered. The clerk was one I had not met before and I explained my problem and my request to exchange them for the proper size. He appeared to be a little perturbed at my request. He looked them over carefully and told me that they had been washed. I assured him that they had not been washed and he continued to insist that they had been. I tried my best to explain to him that I had nothing to gain by lying to him, that I didn't pay for them, the Department had. No matter how I tried to resolve the matter, he continued to insist that I had washed the pants. He pushed them across the counter at me and told me he wasn't taking them back because they had been washed. That was the last time I was going to let the jerk all but call me a liar. I pushed the pants back across the counter and told him to just take them and shove them up his ass! We walked out of the store.

I stopped by the Sheriff's Office and advised the Inspector of the incident. I wanted them to find out from me and I wanted them to know the truth. A few days later I was advised by the Inspector that the Chief Deputy had decided to file an "administrative complaint" against me. I was told that the uniform shop had called and made it clear that they did not want to file a complaint, but wanted to know how they could make it right with me. But this was too good of a chance for the Chief to pass up. He used the situation to harass me even more. I thought "only a rat" like him would take something like this and create a letter of reprimand that would become a part of my file". In 12 years of dedicated service, this would be the only negative thing in my personnel file.

Finally on June 16, 2001, I walked into the Sheriff's Office and handed the Chief Deputy my letter of resignation. As usual, the Sheriff was not around. It was short and simple and to the point, and read as follows:

Please accept this as my letter of resignation, effective immediately. Your administration has made it impossible for me to continue working here.

He was furious and asked if I was sure that was what I wanted to do. I told him I was very sure. I spent about 20 minutes with the Inspector, checking in all the Department issued items. As we carried in the last armload, the Inspector told me the Chief Deputy and Undersheriff wanted to see me before I left. We were standing just outside their office and I told the Inspector loud enough for them to hear, that I wasn't "granting exit interviews." I knew about their so called "exit interviews" and there was no way I would give them the satisfaction of trying to berate me. I also know my own limits. I had started and worked for the Lewis County Sheriff's Office on my terms, and I was determined to leave on my terms. I then walked out, leaving a career behind that I had loved.

I promised the mother of one of the deceased that I would continue to work on the case as a private investigator. During 2000 and 2001, she and I generated so much publicity about her daughter's death, that the Sheriff was forced to reopen the investigation. It was an even bigger joke than the original one, and their efforts to continue to hide the truth became even more evident in their reports. In late 2000, the mother showed me the crime photos that the Sheriff had sent her after two years of requesting them. As I started looking through them, I was shocked at what I saw. There were at least a dozen blank ones that were supposed to be ones that had not developed. None of these blank shots were ever present in 1998. The next few photos explained why. There was a picture of the bedroom, but there was a big difference from when I took photos the morning of the shooting. The photo showed the bed fully made and with a different bedspread. The room was cleaner and more organized. It wasn't until I looked at the next photo that I understood the full impact of what I was seeing. There was a photo of the bathroom mirror. The counter was clearly absent of the items I photographed a few years before. When the mirror was photographed, it reflected onto the photographer giving a clear picture of the person taking the picture. The Detective Sergeant, taking pictures two years after the crime! And to think the Sheriff would go so far as to pass them off to the mother as crime scene photos. Missing were many of the photos that the Deputy, the original Detective, and I took during the original investigation. Missing were the most incriminating pictures, such as the photo with the gun in place before the Detective removed it. Missing were the photos showing the position of the body that were proof that the closet door could not have been closed as was reported. Basically, all she got was a few pictures of the death scene that had been cleaned up and a bunch of blanks, taken two years after the incident. The Sheriff had the State Attorney General Office review the case file. They concluded the death a suicide based on the information the Sheriff's Office provided. Their conclusion was nothing more than that of a couple of former Detectives who were not experts, but who did have a long standing relationship with the Lewis County Sheriff's Office. The Deputy Coroner changed her position under pressure. The Deputy Coroner had a conversation which was recorded by the mother where she was caught telling a lie. The Deputy Coroner was unaware the conversation was being recorded by the mother. Of course, the Prosecutor wanted to pursue a misdemeanor charge against the mother for making the unauthorized recording. There is something wrong when a citizen has to resort to these tactics in order to get to the truth.

    I knew there was little that could be done at this point, but she was never going to let it go. I also promised myself that I would do everything in my power to see that the public came to know the truth about some of the things that really go within their Sheriff's Office. The citizens deserve better than what they have received over the years from the Sheriff's Office Detective Division. I will continue my efforts to inform the citizens of the consequences of a Rotational Detective Program, and the need for a fully qualified and well trained, full time homicide investigator.

After I quit, I didn't waste time in exposing the lack of leadership in the Sheriff's Office by writing letters to the editor of the local newspaper. I openly condemned the Sheriff for his lack of skill and knowledge, the Detective Division for their history of sloppy investigations, and the Rotational Detective Program. Since they couldn't disprove anything I said, they resorted to personal attacks on me through the media. My son, who was still a Deputy with the Department begin to be the target of the Department's anger. It infuriated me to see my son be a target in such a manner, and to me, it spoke volumes of the character of the Sheriff. One evening my son Rowdy called his Sergeant just before the beginning of his shift and told the Sergeant to come get the Patrol car and the rest of the Department's equipment. He quit. One of Sheriff McCroskey's Patrol Sergeants had been encouraging Rowdy to apply for a position with another Police Department in Washington. He was aware of how Rowdy was being treated, and didn't like it. He had even taken Rowdy to the other department and introduced him to the Police Chief. According to the Chief, during part of the testing process, the Sheriff had found out that Rowdy was testing for a position there. He called the Police Chief and started bad mouthing Rowdy, trying to convince the Chief not to hire him. The Sheriff had no way of knowing that Rowdy was right there with the Chief during the call. The Chief later told me that he was well aware of the Sheriff and paid no attention to anything he said. My son was hired and has won several State awards for his service in the Clark County area.

I had lunch with the Police Chief about 2 years after Rowdy was hired and he told me that Rowdy was an excellent Officer, and all he needed when he came there was a little help getting his self esteem built back up after being torn down by the Lewis County Sheriff's Office.

This book could easily be about one case alone, if I were to add everything that has occurred since I quit the Sheriff's Office. However, I am still investigating one suspicious death as a Private Detective.

Since 1998, I have been kept current of the status of one particular case, helping where I could. The mother of the victim has talked with different experts in the medical and forensic fields. New evidence has been submitted to the Sheriff's Office, but they still refuse to step up and do the right thing. In April 2008, KOMO 4 news aired a story on the case. The investigative reporter did a good job and went to great lengths to report the case in a fair manner.

The amazing thing is that all the Sheriff and Coroner would have to do to put this case to rest and satisfy a grieving mother is change the death certificate to homicide. At the very least change it to "undetermined" and the mother of the victim would accept it. It would be a win-win situation for all parties. Why is that so difficult? What are they afraid of?

May 20, 2008, and this case is being set for a judicial review. It has been a long and costly battle for the victim's mother just to have her day in court. If the Court rules in her favor, then the Coroner will be forced by court order to change the death certificate. Perhaps the Sheriff's Office may be ordered to reopen the case for further investigation.

Either one would leave the Sheriff's and Coroner's Offices looking ridiculous, at best.

Authors' Opinions

I HAVE ENDEAVORED to present each case in an objective manner, which will hopefully allow the reader to reach a reasonable conclusion based on factual information. It is my hope that the reader will see an established pattern of less than stellar investigations by the Lewis County Sheriff's Office that reaches back through the years. Worse than an established pattern of what I consider inept and incompetent behavior by the Detective Division, the Sheriff allowed it to continue. This of course is my opinion based on my exposure. The Sheriff, regardless who he or she may be, has the authority, the power, and God knows should posses a moral obligation to the public to provide them with the best services possible.

It wasn't until I left law enforcement and had the opportunity to work with highly trained and educated professionals that I became fully aware of what professionalism really means. The Encarta dictionary describes professionalism as:

1. Professional standards: the skill, competence, or character expected of a member of a highly trained profession.

2. Use of professionals: the use of professionals instead of amateurs.

The professionals I work with practice this concept, and the results are what one would expect from a professional agency. There is a high degree of harmony in the work place, productivity is high, and employees are made to feel like part of the team and the quality of work performed is outstanding. Based on these two simple principles alone, I can state that I never worked with anyone in the Lewis County Sheriff's Office who met theses standards. At last count, there had been over 60 employees leave to seek employment elsewhere.

The Sheriff made much ado about creating a chain gang to punish criminals. What the public didn't really hear much about was that the chain gang was a voluntary program. If an inmate agreed to volunteer, their sentence was reduced by one-third. The upside for the inmate was getting outside for some fresh air, being allowed to smoke cigarettes, and getting their sentence reduced. There really was no downside for them. It did serve as great publicity for the Sheriff and for all purposes, seemed to be a great move toward being tough on criminals. There was much publicity when he announced to the citizens that he was serving the inmates military MRE's (meals ready to eat). Many of the citizens were under the impression that the inmates were eating the MRE's from their original packages same as our military. But I was told by a Correctional Sergeant (name withheld) at the Jail that the military food was ordered in bulk quantities, heated, and served like any other meal.

A lie is a lie, regardless how you color it, and the teller of lies is a liar. History has proven over and over that liars are often cowards who hide behind political power, and often surround themselves with people of like kind. This is a known phenomenon called The Law of Attraction. Just as history shows us, cowards fall in the end and we can take comfort in knowing that history will most likely repeat itself again. Sooner or later, the citizens will wake up and see the tremendous mistakes they have made at the voting booths. They will rise up, as voters often do, and take back control of their County, by voting out leadership that fails to be honest in offices such as County Sheriff's Offices, the Prosecutors Offices and Coroners Offices as well as all elected positions. Lewis County is long overdue professional leadership. We deserve honesty and, most certainly, accountability from our elected officials. As far as I am concerned, those who take County salaries and fail to perform the required duties are nothing less than thieves.

I no longer have any animosity against anyone that was or is associated with the Sheriff's Office. I have apologized to several for the hurt feelings and lost friendships. However, I do not apologize for exposing the truth and for standing by my own convictions. But

I have come to realize that individuals will do what their character and conscience dictates at any given time. Individual standards are self-imposed and each person decides what their own standards will be. Unfortunately, some have much lower standards than others; some quite self-serving regardless of the affect it has on their constituents.

Nothing changes without the involvement of the citizens. When they have had enough and band together for the good of their community, they have the power to set the standards for our elected officials. But only when the citizens are tired of murderers walking free.

ISBN 1425184839